Online with God

Other Books in the growing Faithgirlz!™ library

The Faithgirlz! Bible

My Faithgirlz! Journal

Faithgirlz! Handbook

The Lucy Series

Lucy Doesn't Wear Pink (Book One)

Lucy Out of Bounds (Book Two)

Lucy's "Perfect" Summer (Book Three)

Lucy Finds Her Way (Book Four)

NonFiction

The Skin You're In

Dear Nancy

Body Talk

Girl Politics

Everybody Tells Me to Be Myself but I Don't Know Who I Am

The Sophie Series

Sophie's World (Book One)

Sophie's Secret (Book Two)

Sophie Under Pressure (Book Three)

Sophie Steps Up (Book Four)

Sophie's First Dance (Book Five)

Sophie's Stormy Summer (Book Six)

Sophie's Friendship Fiasco (Book Seven)

Sophie and the New Girl (Book Eight)

Sophie Flakes Out (Book Nine)

Sophie Loves Jimmy (Book Ten)

Sophie's Drama (Book Eleven) Sophie Gets Real (Book Twelve)

Online with God

By Laurie Lazzaro Knowlton

We want to hear from you. Please send your comments about this book to us in care of zreview@zondervan.com. Thank you.

ZONDERKIDZ

Online with God

Requests for information should be addressed to:

Zonderkidz, *Grand Rapids, Michigan 49530*

Library of Congress Cataloging-in-Publication Data

Knowlton, Laurie Lazzaro.
Online with God / by Laurie Lazzaro Knowlton.
p. cm.— (Faithgirlz)
ISBN 978-0-310-71615-0 (softcover)
1. Girls—Prayers and devotions. 2. Girls—Religious life. 3. Girls—Conduct of life.
I. Title.
BV4860.K56 2009
242'.62—dc22 2009020794

Cover design: Sarah Molegraaf
Interior composition and design: Luke Daab and Carlos Eluterio Estrada

Printed in the United States of America

---

10 11 12 13 14 15 16 /DCI/ 21 20 19 18 17 16 15 14 13 12 11 10 9 8 7 6 5 4 3 2 1

IN HONOR OF MY CREATOR,
JESUS CHRIST,
AND FOR RHONDA AND DANDI,
MY CREATIVE WRITING BUDDIES.
ISAIAH 65:18

LLK

DAY 1

Online with God

God Says: There is a time for everything, and a season for every activity under heaven.

Ecclesiastes 3:1

Life is wild. Sometimes it can all be awfully confusing, and other times it's one big party. With all this stuff going on, it's good to have a quiet place to blog about my thoughts, feelings, successes, losses, school, family events, and just plain living. Online with God is my personal blog with my BFF God. This blog isn't going to be candy coated because I know God wouldn't want anything less than the truth.

I'm going to try to post daily. I'm going to keep it small and private, just God and me. It will help me to work through the day's events. Like the Bible says, this is my season to grow and learn how to be a better person. The older I get, the more things change. Like — it's not just going to be my group of friends from elementary anymore. There're kids from all over the city that will be going to this middle school. The kids from my elementary school will be joining with groups from four other schools. I'll met new people and, I hope, make new friends.

Along with friends, school, and living life, I have the usual family stuff. My older sister Melody thinks she's the boss of me. And my parents are still treating me like I'm five. I'd really like to work some of this stuff out so life can be easier for all of us.

The big thing is I'm trying to figure out where I fit. On top of all of that, I know I'm changing, inside and out. I know this is all part of God's plan. So, I guess I'm along for the ride. This blog, Online with God, is going to help me work through all these challenges and changes.

STEPPING UP:

Expressing feelings, concerns, and hopes with God is healthy. He's always going to be the best friend you could ever find. He's a loving, accepting, and forgiving friend. You can trust God during all the craziness life has to serve. The great thing is knowing you never have to face life's changes alone. God is the ultimate BFF.

LET'S TALK:

Dear God, thanks for giving me a place to gather my thoughts and get them down. You are an awesome BFF. I'm totally cool with the changes if you're there to see me through, and I'm blown away that you love me so much. Thanks for being here by my side as I face all the weird stuff out there. There isn't anything I can't face with you by my side. Amen.

DAY 2

I'm Not Listening

God Says: "They were all trying to frighten us, thinking, 'Their hands will get too weak for the work, and it will not be completed.' But I prayed, 'Now strengthen my hands.'"
Nehemiah 6:9

So, I came up with this great idea for writing a blog, and even though it's private I told my friends that I was doing it.

My sister Melody said, "Sweet!" And Olivia said the idea totally rocked. But some of my "friends" asked stuff like "Why bother to blog God if he's always with you?" and "Are you some kind of Jesus freak?"

I'm not going to let them bring me down. They can challenge me all they want, but I'm all about this blog. I'm thinking it must be a good idea if I'm getting reactions from people. Maybe just the fact that I'm blogging will make people take another look at their own relationship with God.

So, to answer the Jesus freak question — maybe I am a Jesus freak, if it means I want to chat with God daily. I'm never alone because God is with me every second of every day. And as far as "Why bother?" No one is looking over my shoulder or making me blog. I write because writing is my thing. A journal is a way to organize my thoughts in this disorganized world, and it's way easier for me to journal online.

So discourage me all you want. I take on the challenge. I'm here to stay, and so is God.

STEPPING UP:

There are two kinds of people in this world. There are people who are filled with discouraging words and a negative outlook, and there are people who are filled with positive words and uplifting energy. Every day you get to make a choice. You can look at the day's challenges and give up, or you can stand up and say, "I can do that!"

LET'S TALK:

Dear God, thank you for the strength to ignore people who challenge our time together. Help me to organize my thoughts and make good choices, and help me to keep from doubting all the time I spend with you. Amen.

DAY 3

To Go or Not to Go

God Says: Ask where the good way is, and walk in it, and you will find rest for your souls.

Jeremiah 6:16

So, Emma just had a birthday party. I was invited, but Olivia wasn't. This has happened before, and I usually find a way to get an invite for her too, since she's my BFF and everything. People just don't understand her like I do. See, she's gorgeous, but she's also shy. People think she's a snob, but she's so not into herself like that.

In reality Olivia's very much like me, except the beautiful part. I just don't fall under the gorgeous umbrella. I'd describe myself as average other than being short. I have long brown hair and brown eyes. My friends on the cheerleader squad say I'm cute and bubbly, but I know they would never describe me as GORGEOUS.

Anyway, just because Olivia's not outgoing doesn't make her a snob. She's totally kind and funny. She loves horses, just like me. She loves to cook — mostly gooey desserts. And I've gone to her family's cottage every summer. Olivia has been my BFF for years.

When I emailed Emma back accepting her invitation, I asked if I could bring Olivia. Emma totally freaked and said I was trying to ruin her party — it was just for cheerleaders. I responded that I had no intention of ruining her party and that she would like Olivia if she would just give her a chance.

Again, Emma told me the invite was for cheerleaders and cheerleaders ONLY.

I decided that I didn't want to attend a party where I would have to worry about freaking out Emma. I told her thanks for the invite, but I wouldn't be able to make it after all. But I hated to have to miss the party. God, was that the right thing to do?

STEPPING UP:

Being a good friend means all the time, not just when it's easy or convenient. Loyalty is one of the greatest responsibilities and most valuable gifts God has given us. How can you show loyalty to your best friend?

LET'S TALK:

Father, it's hard when friends you care about don't care for each other. Why can't everyone get along? Help me to be an example of your love, understanding, and acceptance. Teach me to be a good friend. Amen.

DAY 4

Who Is That Green-Eyed Monster?

God Says: Therefore, as God's chosen people, holy and dearly loved, clothe yourselves with compassion, kindness, humility, gentleness and patience.

Colossians 3:12

School starts in a week. I've been saving my babysitting money all summer for an awesome new outfit to wear on the first day of school. So today was the big day to go shopping My whole cheerleading squad — Emma, Brittany, Samantha, Trudy, and Chloe — met at the mall. We went from store to store, trying on a gazillion outfits. Samantha snapped pictures the whole time for her blog, like we were having a major fashion show.

The thing is that when most of the girls try on an outfit, they look like real models. But I'm short and the clothes are always way too long. I have to shorten everything, except for miniskirts, and those hit me like a regular skirt should.

The more we tried on clothes, the more I could feel this jealousy monster raging inside. I was jealous that the other girls had their parents' credit cards and could buy, buy, buy.

I was jealous that everything they put on looked fantastic on them, but totally hideous on me. I was jealous when Samantha's pictures for her blog made everyone look like cover models, especially Trudy, and I looked like someone in hand-me-downs.

I thought I kept my feelings to myself. I tried. But looking at Samantha's blog tonight, the pictures practically shout what a jealous brat I am. I don't like that person in the pictures.

I'm off to Samantha's to tell her I'm sorry for feeling jealous and ask her to take down the pictures. I hope she'll understand.

STEPPING UP:

Never post pictures of someone that are not uplifting. Pictures on the Internet can take on a life of their own and can end up anywhere. If someone has posted a picture of you that you would prefer to keep private, talk to the person who uploaded it and ask if it can be removed.

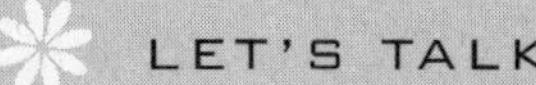

LET'S TALK:

Lord, help me to stay clothed in kindness and humility so that I can be a better friend and a better me. Thanks, God. Amen.

DAY 5

I'm Chillin'

God Says: A fool gives full vent to his anger, but a wise man keeps himself under control.

Proverbs 29:11

Brittany and I were supposed to work at the library for the summer reading club finale. We're finishing up our volunteer hours for church.

I called her, like, a million times and she never returned my call. I thought maybe she forgot to charge her cell and I decided I'd stop by her house so we could walk over together. No one was home when I got to her house. I started to worry that maybe something happened. So I text messaged her and left a message on her house phone.

I headed over to the library because I didn't want to be late. Brittany wasn't there either. The library was a madhouse. I think every kid in the elementary school was jammed in the children's department for story hour. I definitely had trouble working crowd control, and we really could have used Brittany's help. The librarian kept thanking me for being there and asking where Brittany was. Like I should know.

Later, Brittany and a bunch of other girls were in the school chat room talking about the boys they met at the movies. Brittany totally bailed on me! I can't believe she blew off her volunteer job. She's the one who signed me up to volunteer with her. The first time she gets something better to do, she takes off. Not a word to me or the library. And tonight she had the nerve to text message me like nothing happened! I could really let her have it!

STEPPING UP:

It's always better to cool off before you respond to someone who has upset you — especially if you're responding online or in a text message. Once you've chilled out, ask your friend if you can talk. A real friend is someone who understands the true meaning of commitments — both to her responsibilities and to you.

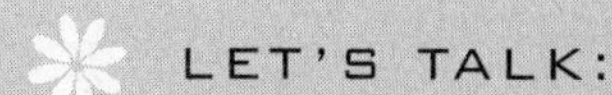

LET'S TALK:

Lord, when I'm angry help me to think about what you would do. Remind me to think before opening my mouth, and help me to be a forgiving friend. Amen.

DAY 6

It Was an Itsy Bitsy Teenie Weenie Pink Polka-Dot Tankini

God Says: Listen to advice and accept instruction, and in the end you will be wise.

Proverbs 19:20

Pool Party! I was dreading going to the pool and meeting all my friends with my old, faded, getting-too-small swimsuit. Mom took one look at how tight it was and said we could go shopping for a new suit, even though it's the end of summer. I was so excited. I found a strapless yellow tankini with tiny pink flowers. My mother was absolutely against a strapless yellow suit. She said the top might slip down, or the suit might be too light in color. We compromised, and I got a polka-dot pink suit with a neck strap.

Later I met Olivia at the pool. We were watching the boys doing flips off the board, the lifeguards flexing, and the high school girls trying to command the spotlight. We chilled, soaking up the rays, loving the last days of summer and the pool.

Then we went for a swim. When I climbed out of the pool, Olivia gasped and pointed at me. My new bathing suit was, like, almost totally see-through. I was on display for anyone looking my way. I grabbed my towel, covered up, and ran for the locker room.

Olivia kept saying no one saw me. She said everyone was busy checking out her brother Jack and Brittany's poolside romance. It didn't matter. No way was I going back out to the pool. I headed home.

Later I found out that someone had seen me and photographed my most embarrassing moment with their cell phone. Now my unveiled self has been emailed to some of my friends.

STEPPING UP:

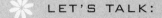

Not knowing who posted personal pictures on the Internet can make you feel violated and out of control of your life. If you discover that pictures of you have been posted or made public without your permission, talk to a parent or trusted adult immediately.

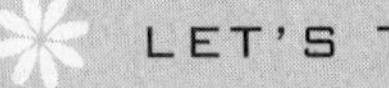

LET'S TALK:

My loving Father, I know there isn't anything you and my parents can't help me work out. Help me to rely on them and you to keep me safe. Thank you for your unending love. Amen.

Walking with You

God Says: When I am afraid, I will trust you. In God, whose word I praise, in God I trust; I will not be afraid. What can mortal man do to me?

Psalm 56:3 – 4

First day of school is tomorrow, and I can't sleep. I guess I'm nervous about all my classes. I've had those nightmares about not remembering my locker combination, or starting my period in the middle of gym, or being late for a class. Then there is the nightmare about getting ditched by my friend in front of everyone. It all makes my stomach hurt.

Speaking of stomachs, who am I going to eat lunch with? I checked my schedule online and then called a few of my friends. As far as I can tell, I don't have lunch with anyone I know. I hope I'm not going to be a loser sitting all by myself! If only I could just relax.

I'm going to study the school map and look at my schedule online again and try to remember the room numbers, my teachers' names, my locker number and combination. I hate numbers. There are too many numbers here!

I'm a total mess. I need to relax. Think of something happy. Think. Think. Think.

Augh! It's no use! I know it all sounds like I'm spazzing out – it's just the way I am whenever I start something new. I wish it were next week already! Then I would be past the first day and I'd be just fine.

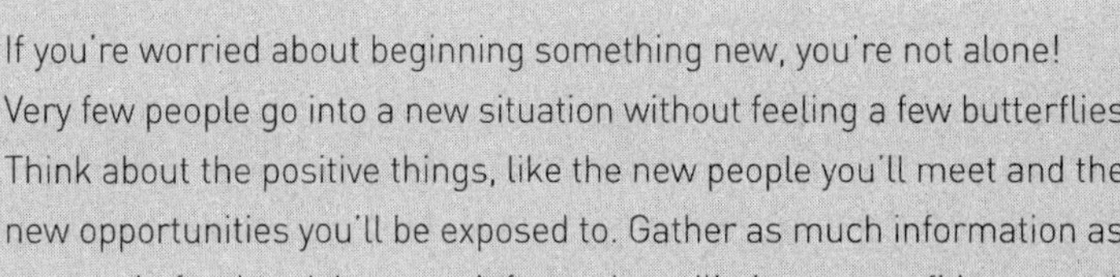

STEPPING UP:

If you're worried about beginning something new, you're not alone! Very few people go into a new situation without feeling a few butterflies. Think about the positive things, like the new people you'll meet and the new opportunities you'll be exposed to. Gather as much information as you can beforehand, because information will give you confidence, and confidence heads off worry.

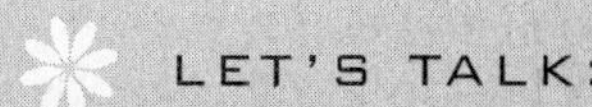

LET'S TALK:

Lord, I wonder if you were ever scared about going to any of the new towns where you traveled to preach. Whenever I get nervous, I'm going to hang onto the fact that you are there with me, every step of the way. I ask for your peace to fill all the spaces in my head that are wiggling with worry. Help me to walk confidently knowing you are walking beside me. Amen.

DAY 8

Not It

God Says: Cast your cares on the Lord and he will sustain you.

Psalm 55:22

I am so bummed! The list is posted and I didn't make the cut. I don't get why I didn't make the cheerleading team. I was on the squad last year in middle school. I know I'm not the best tumbler, but I try really hard. Why didn't I take some classes over the summer to improve my tumbling?

The coach says she's all about her squad not only being great cheerleaders but also being wholesome girls who are good examples to the student body. I've always tried to be the best person I could be.

I really loved being a cheerleader. Now I'm going to be sitting on the sidelines, alone. Most of my closest friends are on the squad. Every night they'll be busy with practice. Every Friday they'll be at the game. My whole social life is down the tubes, and no one seems to care. They're all going around, like, in cheerleader heaven, and I am totally invisible, forgotten, and alone.

I checked the school website, and their names and pictures are posted all over the place. They all have quotes like, "We rock! Best friends forever!"

"Cheer! C-Cheer, H-Happily, E-Eagerly, E-Expressively, R-Resoundingly!"

But all I can see is that I am missing from those pictures. They're all together, and I'm ALONE. A-Absent, L-Lonely, O-Outcast, N-Nerd, E-Evicted. What am I going to do now?

STEPPING UP:

Not being chosen to be part of a group can be a hard blow to your self-confidence. The thing to remember is that one activity does not sum up who you are. You have many talents, interests, and friends that will help you discover more about God and more about yourself.

LET'S TALK:

Father, sometimes I feel really lost and alone, without friends who really understand what I'm going through. Help me to remember that you have awesome plans for me, no matter what happens. Bring people into my life that will bring me closer to you and your glory. Amen.

DAY 9 Being In on the IM

God Says: So in everything, do to others what you would have them do to you.

Matthew 7:12

My friends always meet in our chat room every Thursday at 9:00 p.m. It started out with us talking about school, the football game, and how awful the cafeteria food tastes. Now there are like a gazillion people in the chat room every Thursday.

It used to be fun, but now I dread Thursdays. Our talks start off harmless enough, and then someone's name gets brought up. The minute a person's name is mentioned everyone starts dissing them. They put down their looks, their clothes, their grades, and their families. Everything you never needed to know about that person is posted and dissected.

Well, last Thursday I tried to stop the attack by saying we are better than that. Then all of a sudden I started reading nasty comments about me! I responded by telling them that they needed to stop and think about how they would feel if people were being nasty to them. Someone wrote "LOL," and it just got worse. None of my friends from the squad even bothered to stand up for me. I turned off my computer, not caring if I ever got back on.

I couldn't believe it. The next day at school people treated me like I was invisible. The only person who talked to me all day was the girl I stood up for. But I was so upset about being bashed that I snapped at her. I really wish I hadn't ever been a part of the Thursday chat room.

STEPPING UP:

Speaking up when someone is under attack is a very difficult thing to do, but it's the right thing to do. Bullies enjoy the thrill of getting a reaction, so ignore them. If the meanness continues, make copies of every hurtful IM, email, or text message you receive for evidence. Then take the information to a parent or a teacher.

LET'S TALK:

Dear Lord, sometimes standing up for what's right hurts more than just staying quiet. So, I thank you, God, for giving me the strength to listen to what you say to do. I trust you, Lord, and know you'll take care of me. Amen.

DAY 10

TMI

God Says: Dear friend, do not imitate what is evil but what is good.

3 John 11

I got a photo of Blake on my cell phone while I was walking to lunch today. I've known Blake since first grade. He's a really nice guy, but the photo didn't share that. It zeroed in on his naked stomach, hanging below his shirt. It didn't help that Blake was inhaling a candy bar.

When I entered the lunchroom, it was total chaos, with kids looking at their cell phones and laughing. Text messages were flying from phone to phone — "Look what caf food can do for you!" "Eat chocolate for a bigger, better you!" or "Feeling bloated? Eat less!"

Blake walked in seconds later, and the whole cafeteria burst out laughing. He looked around to see what people were laughing at, and when he realized they were all looking at him, he checked to see if his fly was open. The more he tried to figure out what was so funny, the worse it got. People were practically falling over they were laughing so hard. Then Josh handed Blake a candy bar, and everyone went crazy.

The cafeteria lady blew her whistle and made everyone stop and eat in silence. I was glad she stopped the laughter. Blake wouldn't hurt a fly. I don't think I'll ever forget the look on his face when he realized the joke was on him. He left the cafeteria without eating lunch. I didn't feel much like eating mine either. I went to look for him at break but couldn't find him anywhere.

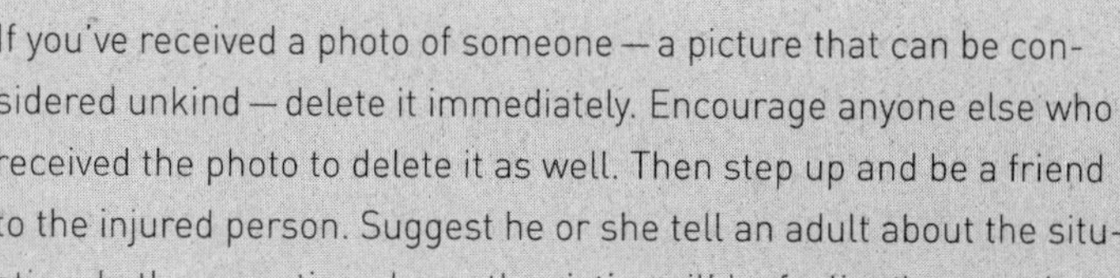

STEPPING UP:

If you've received a photo of someone — a picture that can be considered unkind — delete it immediately. Encourage anyone else who received the photo to delete it as well. Then step up and be a friend to the injured person. Suggest he or she tell an adult about the situation. In the meantime, know the victim will be feeling hurt, embarrassed, and alone. Let that person know you care.

LET'S TALK:

Father, help me to be a friend to the Blakes of this world. Give me the courage to stand up when I see kids being cruel and give me the wisdom to deal with the situation responsibly. Thanks, God. Amen.

What Not to Model

God Says: We all, like sheep, have gone astray.

Isaiah 53:6

I have gotten totally hooked on a TV show — Model Search. I know it's stupid. It all started when I was helping take care of my grandmother last summer. She watched Model Search religiously. She could tell you about each girl like she knew them personally. She'd talk to the models like they could hear her when she told them, "Stop putting on so much make-up" or "A.J., you have to eat something! You're going to starve to death!"

When school started I couldn't watch the show anymore, and I didn't think about it much until I was at the grocery store and saw a magazine with big headlines: "Top Ten Models Duke It Out for Number One!!" That's what grabbed my attention.

My favorite model made it to the top ten. So, I started watching the show at night online. I never had to miss an episode — I could pull them up on the web anytime after the show aired.

Now I'm totally addicted. I know, I know—addictions are never good, especially to a television show. It's not like I don't have enough drama in my own life. I justify watching because when I call Grandma we have something to talk about. But truthfully, I'm not so sure the show's good for me to be watching all the time. I see those perfect women up on stage and wish so much that I could look like them. I've gotten pretty insecure about my body, my hair, my clothes ... and I don't think that's what God wants for me.

STEPPING UP:

There isn't much on TV that you would feel comfortable watching with Jesus. And yet most of America is hooked on a daytime or night-time show that includes adultery, lying, cheating, and breaking many of God's laws. You can find things to do that are good, healthy uses of your free time. Learn how to cook a favorite meal or ask your mom if you can work on scrapbooking old family pictures. Spend time with your family instead of draining it away in front of a screen, and you'll feel better about yourself instead of criticizing the beautiful young woman God made.

LET'S TALK:

Dear Father, I've seen how unholy some television shows can be. Please don't let this world suck me into its garbage. You have given me and this world so many opportunities to make good choices. Thanks for always giving me a fresh chance to make choices that are pleasing to you. Amen.

DAY 12

Belonging

God Says: You also are among those who are called to belong to Jesus Christ.

Romans 1:6

Ever since last week when I got slammed by everyone in the chat room I haven't written a word in my public blog. In school I feel like I'm looking over my shoulder for the other shoe to drop. All of this only seems to point out my feelings of not belonging. Like there isn't a place for me. Everyone seems to belong somewhere: cheerleading, football, choir, the band, the drama club, and the list goes on.

I feel like I'm standing outside a window watching all the kids inside have a life. People pass me in halls talking and laughing, and I walk around wondering where I fit. I used to be a cheerleader. I used to know where I belonged.

I know I should count my blessings. It's not like the girls from my elementary school squad aren't still nice to me when I see them. I'm also my homeroom's student council representative. There are people that say "Hi!" to me in the halls. I guess I'm just not feeling sure of myself. I look in the mirror and I see me, but I don't feel like me.

God, I sure could use some guidance. I don't want to keep feeling like a fish out of water.

STEPPING UP: 

Everyone goes through times where they feel like they don't belong. Even homecoming queens sometimes wonder where they fit. To belong you have to like yourself. If you like yourself, people will see your confidence, and confidence is attractive. Confidence begins when you take the time to claim the gifts God gave you. When you accept who you are, you'll see that you don't feel so alone and insecure. You belong to the family of God!

 LET'S TALK:

Dear Lord, please help me not to get bummed about where I belong or don't belong. Let me feel confident in who you made me to be. But most of all help me to remember I do belong—I belong to you. I am your chosen child. You picked me to be on your squad. How cool is that! Amen.

DAY 13

Roller Coaster Feelings

God Says: Do not arouse or awaken love until it so desires.
Song of Songs 2:7

I have a total crush on Olivia's brother, Jack. He was hanging out with Brittany until Labor Day. Jack's a few years older, plays drums in the band, and has really great hair. I never thought about him much until the end of the summer.

Our middle school and high school are on the same campus. They're sharing the middle school's cafeteria and gym this year while the high school is getting renovated. Now I get to see Jack every day.

Jack and his friends sit at a table near ours. Yesterday I totally ran into him at the vending machines. For just a second our hands touched. We both reached out at the same time to put our change in the candy bar machine. I wasn't paying attention and neither was he, because he looked as surprised as I did. Well, when I looked up into his dark brown eyes, I almost melted like a chocolate bar on a hot summer day. The problem is that he couldn't care less about me.

I asked my older sister, Melody, to look online for Jack's profile. He had all the usual stuff, a list of his likes and dislikes. I think I've memorized every word. He had pictures of his favorite band, pictures of him and his friends playing street hockey, and some pictures of his family camping in the woods.

I've totally fallen for him. I am wishing for a miracle that will make him fall for me too.

STEPPING UP:

Crushes are always exciting — especially a first crush. Be careful, though, not to mistake that fluttery feeling for love. Love is based on time spent getting to know a person and finding things in common that you both value. Check out 1 Corinthians 13 — the famous "love chapter." That's the kind of love that God has planned for you someday. There will be some confusion and heartbreak along the way, but keeping focused on God and his will for your life will keep the path to love smooth.

LET'S TALK:

Dear God, this liking-a-boy stuff is so confusing. How can I feel so happy just because a guy looks at me, then so crushed because he doesn't even seem to know who I am? Lord, please help me figure this whole boy-girl thing out, and help me to wait on your time. Amen.

DAY 14

Who's Missing?

God Says: For we cannot help speaking about what we have seen and heard.

Acts 4:20

Thank goodness for student council. I know it's lame, but at least I'm not totally out of the loop. I'm even kicking around the idea of running for class president.

The odd thing about student council is that most of us also attend the same youth group at church. And that's what got me thinking about tonight's entry.

All of the student council reps met in the school online chat room to plan the tailgate party before the football game. Each of the student council representatives heads a committee. We have an advertising committee, a decorations committee, a food committee, and a music committee. Samantha thought a slideshow of our team players shown on the outside school wall would be a great addition. We all agreed. Everyone's sick of pizza and hot dogs, so Rachel's idea of having a submarine sandwich the same size and shape as the goal post was a big success. The sub sandwiches got us thinking of the theme, and then someone suggested a whole nautical/submarine thing for decorations. Our rivals for this game are the Pirates, so Chloe said she could illustrate some signs saying, "Sink the Pirates!" with illustrations of our team running torpedoes into ships.

Later a few of us from youth group were still online. We talked about school, student council, and spirit committee, but never once did we talk God. It seems wrong — you know? We should be talking about God as naturally outside youth group as we do inside youth group.

STEPPING UP:

It's a good thing to notice when you've boxed God into certain times and places. You need to take God out of the box and invite him to be part of your everyday life. He's already walking with you. Now you need to walk with him.

LET'S TALK:

Thank you, Father, when you open my eyes and help me see that I need to make some changes. I want to make you part of everything. Thank you for thinking about me each minute of every day. I'm working on catching up with you. Amen.

DAY 15

Horsing Around

God Says: A righteous man cares for the needs of his animal.

Proverbs 12:10

I desperately want to have a horse, but we live in the suburbs. No horses for miles and miles around. Mom takes Olivia and me riding at a stable about an hour away from us one Saturday every month. I love going there. Every time I go I feel like I'm in horse heaven. I love the smell of horses. I love to hear their gentle nickers, and I love to ride. I think horses and dogs are God's perfect animals. Besides writing my blog, riding is the only place where I can think and work things out. It's quality time with God's most beautiful animal, nature, and me. Olivia feels the same way.

That's why I was totally sick at heart when I saw on the news that twelve horses had to be rescued from a stable where they had been left to starve. These poor horses' ribs were sticking out. Their heads hung low, and their eyes were all watery. What kind of person could do such a thing? I mean, I was totally crying for these poor abused horses. I knew I needed to get involved.

The newscaster gave a website where they would post the horses' progress back to health. The rescuers asked for donations. They said you could "adopt" one of the horses and they'd send you emails with personal information on the horse you adopted. I was so excited! I could finally, sort of, adopt a horse!

I called Olivia and we decided we were going to get involved. She came over, and we looked up the website to find out what we needed to do.

STEPPING UP:

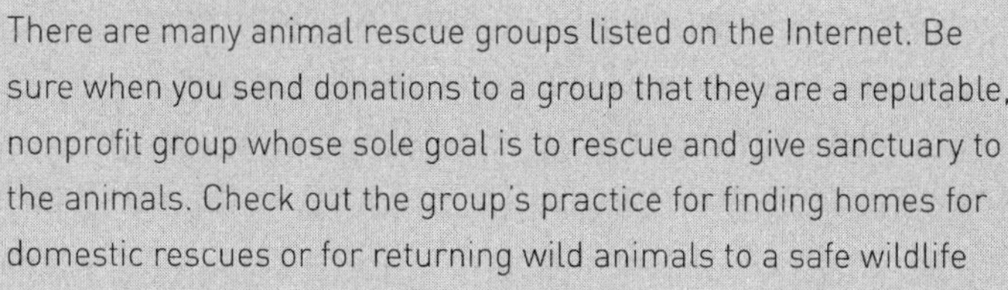

There are many animal rescue groups listed on the Internet. Be sure when you send donations to a group that they are a reputable, nonprofit group whose sole goal is to rescue and give sanctuary to the animals. Check out the group's practice for finding homes for domestic rescues or for returning wild animals to a safe wildlife preserve.

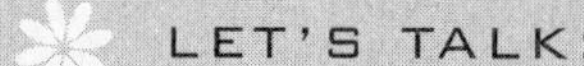

LET'S TALK:

Dear God, I can only imagine how heartbroken you must be when you see your glorious creatures being neglected. God, please stir the hearts of humanity to take better care of your precious creations. Amen.

Horse Cents

God Says: Hope deferred makes the heart sick, but a longing fulfilled is a tree of life.

Proverbs 13:12

My two horse-crazy friends, Olivia and Blake, and I held a carwash. We asked for donations and had pictures of the horses. People were great! We were able to collect $416.67. We counted every penny — even the three cents we found on the ground. We sent all the money to the horse rescue. Now we are "foster parents" of three of the rescue horses! We get emails every day with an update on Star, Socks, and Max. Even though I can't go and see them in person or groom them, I am so happy to finally, sort of, own a horse. It just feels good knowing I helped save a horse's life.

Olivia and Blake said that maybe we could just keep our change and send more money every week. It is amazing how a few cents here and there add up. I even got Dad, Mom, and Melody to throw their change in at the end of the day.

It is a wonderful thing to have wanted a horse and now to finally have a way to help a horse. I've realized some important things as a result of becoming a foster parent for Star, Socks, and Max. I guess you could call it my Horse Cents. It takes money, time, and care to have a horse. I've realized that you appreciate some things more if you have to wait. I've also come to realize owning a horse isn't all about me and what I get. It is about what the horse needs. It's all been a joyful eye-opener.

STEPPING UP:

It can be hard — if not downright impossible — to wait for something you really want. But while we wait we learn, and when you're finally ready to get what you've been waiting for it's even better! If you're in a waiting time right now, what might the Lord be teaching you?

LET'S TALK:

Dear Father, thank you for every blessing you've already brought into my life and for all the prayers you've answered. As I'm waiting for other blessings to come into my life, give me the patience and the peace to rely on your perfect time. Amen.

DAY 17

Birthday Blues

God Says: A man of many companions may come to ruin, but there is a friend who sticks closer than a brother.

Proverbs 18:24

Next Saturday is my birthday. I sent out these totally cool invites I found online. They have little squirrels jumping around shaking acorns saying, "Come to my birthday and let's get a little nuts!" I sent them out to a bunch of people from school, telling them we were going to my grandparents' campgrounds. I asked everyone to bring their sleeping bags and outdoor clothes. I thought it was a really cool and unique party.

Well, within the last few hours I've had three people email me back asking if they were going to have to sleep outside, on the ground. Two others crabbed about the outhouse. I even had one girl whine about eating hot dogs.

I wrote back, telling them we were going to have a monster bonfire and tell scary stories. I told them that my mom and grandma made mouth-watering baked Alaska in the hot coals. I told them that my dad would be there playing his guitar. And I topped it off saying that he told the scariest ghost stories.

But it seemed the more I tried to convince them the more my friends totally bailed. Sure, they made up excuses, but they were just about as lame as the people who made them. The only three friends who said they would come were Olivia, Rachel, and Chloe.

STEPPING UP:

A party is a pretty big deal. And it hurts when people you call friends bail on you. What you need to realize is that your real friends will be there. Most people only ever have a handful of true friends in their lifetime. All other acquaintances come and go. Cherish your real friends and keep them close to you.

LET'S TALK:

Dear Father, parties can be a setup for a downfall. Help me to focus on what I do have — friends and family who value me for who I am. Help me to cherish them as well and enjoy the memories I can make with them. Amen.

DAY 18

Choices

God Says: Do not fret because of evil men or be envious of the wicked.

Proverbs 24:19

I found out that the reason no one wanted to come to my party was because Josh was having a party the same night. His older cousin was watching him while his parents were away. All the cool kids were there, and I even heard a rumor that there was beer.

So while Olivia, Rachel, Chloe, and I were drinking hot cider and making baked Alaska with my mom and grandma, half the school was downing beer and pretzels. Last week I was so disappointed, upset, and kind of jealous.

Man, am I glad now! You see, we had a blast at my party. We saw shooting stars. We heard a pair of great horned owls calling back and forth to each other. We sang and laughed until way late in the night. But the totally jaw-dropping coolest thing was that we saw the northern lights. Seriously!

It was about three o'clock in the morning. My dog Charlie started barking. I was so tired I told him to come lay down. But he wouldn't stop. Then we saw them. The northern lights! They looked like a pale purple sheet flapping across the sky. The color would simmer from pale purple to misty white then a hazy blue-green. This went on for over an hour. Dad said he didn't know that the northern lights could be seen this far south. Grandma said they used to see them more often before all the light pollution. When I think about the miraculous light show we were able to see I feel so sorry for all the kids at the party who thought they needed beer to have fun.

STEPPING UP:

God is able to see the whole picture: yesterday, today, tomorrow. Because we can't do this, he gave us a guide book, the Bible. The Bible helps us to make godly choices when we're faced with difficult decisions.

LET'S TALK:

Dear Father, thank you for the chance to enjoy your love and beauty. Help me to remember your love when I have tough choices to make. Amen.

DAY 19

It's a Sign!

God Says: Trust in the Lord with all your heart and lean not on your own understanding; in all your ways acknowledge him, and he will make your paths straight.
Proverbs 3:5–6

We were hanging out at Samantha's today, and she started reading everyone's horoscope off the Internet. Everyone stopped talking and started hanging onto every word she was reading like it was Gospel truth.

Samantha rattled off information about the zodiac signs. She showed us pictures of what each one looked like and the dates that surrounded each sign. Then she totally confused me by talking about how signs change according to the moon. It was like the myths we learned about in social studies last year.

But then my friends started giving Samantha their birth dates. So Samantha looked up their date and then read them their horoscope. She said Rachel needed to lay low until the thirteenth because the moon was in the wrong phase for good things to happen. Then she told Brittany she was going to lose someone dear to her by the tenth. Emma was going to be popular with the boys, and Chloe was going to fall into some unexpected money.

I couldn't believe what I was seeing. Rachel started looking over her shoulder like a boulder was going to fall on her head any minute. Brittany started calling her family, warning them of impending doom. Emma got this flirty look in her eyes and said, "Look out boys! Emma's on the prowl." Chloe had her hand out like money was going to miraculously appear in her palm.

I was totally blown away. Why would they believe in Samantha's horoscope when they know the only truths come from the Bible?

STEPPING UP:

The Internet can be a wonderful source of information. It can also be a source of temptations. You know God is in charge of your future. When you have a question, refer to God's Word. The answers are there.

LET'S TALK:

Heavenly Father, thank you for knowing all things about me. Help me to trust in you, and you alone. Also, please help me to have the strength to stand up for your truths to my friends. Lord, help me to remember that you see all things, and you are in control. Amen.

DAY 20

Hoaxed

God Says: Do not spread false reports. Do not help a wicked man by being a malicious witness.

Exodus 23:1

I got one of those Internet hoaxes today. It had big headlines: "MP3 Player Causes Lightning Strike Death!" The article said MP3 players and cell phones will attract lightning from the storm directly to strike the user.

As I read the article, I started to wonder if it could possibly be true. I know there are all kinds of hoaxes that circulate. Like the one about some company sending one hundred dollars to every person receiving the email, as long as they're willing to pass it on to at least ten people. So I decided I'd ask my parents.

Together we looked up Snopes.com. Dad says it is a resource used to expose rumors. Sure enough, it was there among like a million other weird rumors. It had a list of hoaxes invented to tie up the Internet and frighten the reader. Together, Dad and I found a whole article about the lightning, and the facts were different from the email I got. It's false that lightning seeks people on the phone or using an MP3 player. The facts are that if you're using one of those items, the lightning has an electronic conductor directly through the wires to your head and ears. It was recommended to avoid the use of these items if caught in a storm.

I wish I understood why people bend the truth to try to scare people. At least now I know where to go to find the truth when I get an email that sounds like a hoax.

STEPPING UP:

It's wise to check out forwards containing emergency-type information. One way is to contact the original sender. The other is to check out one of the many urban legend or hoax sites. These sites will inform you of false stories that are making the rounds via the Internet.

LET'S TALK:

Lord, I'm not sure why people do things to try and get people wound up. I guess it makes them feel powerful. How sad it is that they can't feel the power of living a Christ-filled life. Father, I ask that you fill them with your spirit and love. I also ask that you help the innocent people receiving this garbage to see it for what it is and not get upset or worried. I'm all about finding my strength in you. Amen.

DAY 21 Never Better

God Says: Turn your ear to me, come quickly to my rescue.

Psalm 31:2

The whole thing with me liking Jack has gotten completely out of control. Olivia kept bugging me, asking if I liked her brother. She emailed, asking. She text messaged me, asking. And last night she asked while we were in the chat room. She put it out there for everyone to read. I was so embarrassed. I wrote back and said that I would never go out with her geek of a brother. What was I thinking?

Immediately every headline on every chat, IM, email, and forum going around school is about me and Jack. Except there never was a "me and Jack." This is too embarrassing! Why did I ever respond? Or, if I had to respond, why didn't I say, "Doesn't everyone like your brother?" I could have answered a million better ways than calling her brother a geek. I never do well with quick answers. This is a nightmare!

Today Olivia won't even talk to me. And at lunch the boys at Jack's table were saying stuff like, "Hey Jack! There's your girlfriend — NOT!" They all were laughing and, worst of all, Jack's glare could have killed me on the spot.

I grabbed my lunch and went down to Mrs. Dobson's room. I told her I wanted to finish working on my science project. But that was only a temporary safety zone. The minute the bell rang, the teasing and laughter started again. I'm never going to live this down.

STEPPING UP:

Guy-girl exchanges made on the net seem to take on a life of their own. As hard as it is when you're in the throes of an exchange, you're better off not to say or write anything, rather than to do so and then have to live with the results. The good news is that tomorrow is a new day. Sadly, someone else will be in the headlines. Think of how you can step up and be a friend to the next headliner.

LET'S TALK:

Dear Father, please help me to remember that if I don't know what to say or do in an online situation I can just sign off. Help me not to say things that hurt, but things that will build up others. Thank you for standing by me in every situation. Amen.

DAY 22

The Right Thing

God Says: The man of integrity walks securely, but he who takes crooked paths will be found out.

Proverbs 10:9

I love to write. I write stories, poems, and cards to my family and friends. My brain just works that way. I hear people in my class complaining when our teacher gives us a writing assignment, but I can't wait to get started. A lot of times my teacher even reads my stuff in class.

Like a few days ago, we were asked to write a description of fall. How simple is that? Write a few words about the colors, add something about the crisp fall breeze, and finish up with the smell of burning leaves.

That evening, while writing my homework, I get an IM from Josh. He tells me how much he admires my writing. Then he asks me for help. My parents have always said that we should share our talents. But by the time we were finished, I practically wrote every word for him. He was so thankful that I tried not to let it bother me.

Today, he IM'd me about how pumped his parents were when he brought home an A on his paper. Then Josh asked for help on our assignment to interview a grandparent. Never mind that he's ignored me since I helped him with the first paper.

I messaged him saying that I would give him some suggestions, but I wasn't going to write the paper for him again. Josh shot back saying he wrote that paper. So I told him, "Great! You can write this one by yourself too."

I'm still mad at myself for being manipulated into doing the work on his first paper. And I'm mad at him for scamming me. I'm having trouble respecting myself and him.

STEPPING UP: 

There's a fine line between helping someone and actually doing all the work. God expects each of us to honor him through the work that we accomplish. When we complete someone else's work, we rob them of the opportunity to learn and we compromise our own integrity.

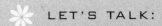

LET'S TALK:

God, when someone asks me for help, show me how to do so while honoring you. Help me to have respect for myself and others when I work. Amen.

DAY 23

We're All Human

God Says: But Jesus would not entrust himself to them, for he knew all men. He did not need man's testimony about man, for he knew what was in a man.

John 2:24 – 25

Mr. Frank has always been one of my favorite youth group leaders. He remembers what it's like to be a kid. He's always joking around with us, and he makes our discussions so much better because he gets us. He comes dressed up like different Bible characters. He adds this totally off-the-wall stuff that always brings us back to the lesson without making us feel like we just sat through a sermon. Like the week he was talking to us about joy. He brought this giant bottle of Joy dishwashing soap, and every time he said "joy" the bottle would send bubbles floating in the air.

Anyway, this weekend while he was at a football game, he was arrested for drunk driving. I don't get it. He's always talking to us about being responsible. He told us that drinking was a dead-end street, and that only losers needed booze to feel good. So what was he thinking?

Josh's dad is a lawyer and got Mr. Frank out. Josh sent an email to a friend, who forwarded it to a couple of other kids, and now everyone knows. But worse than that, everyone is totally dissing Mr. Frank. I'm pretty disappointed in him too, but also in all the rumors that are flying around. I don't think Jesus would want us to be acting like this.

STEPPING UP:

It is very hard when someone you look up to blows it or makes a mistake. Remember, no one is flawless — even the people we admire. Jesus told us that only a person free of sin has the right to judge. Since none of us is sin free, we are called to be forgiving.

LET'S TALK:

Dear Father, It's hard to understand when people fail to live up to their talk. I ask that you help us keep your golden rule. Help me to be forgiving. Amen.

God Listens

God Says: In my distress I called to the Lord; I cried to my God for help. From his temple he heard my voice; my cry came before him, into his ears.

Psalm 18:6

Our church has this really great listserve. Every family in our congregation gets a daily list of prayer requests that have been brought before our community. Every night before dinner, Dad, Mom, Melody, and I check the requested prayers, and we lift up each request when we say grace. This has been a really great way to see answered prayer. Our prayer requests aren't always answered in the way we had hoped — that's been the hardest part to understand. Dad says God knows what he's doing, and who are we to question God?

We haven't ever put a prayer request out to the community except when Grandma Dolly had to go in the hospital. The prayer response was great. Grandma got cards from people in the congregation who remembered her from when she visited us in the summer. Grandma recovered quickly, and she said she was sure it was because of all the prayers said for her.

Well, the other day I asked for prayers for Olivia's family. Her Dad has been transferred and they are going to have to move when their house sells. I'm heartbroken, and so is Olivia's family. Even though it will take time for their house to sell, the day will come when she is going to be gone. What will I do without Olivia?

The listserve responded saying that they only post critical issues. Otherwise the server would be overwhelmed with less important issues. I was practically knocked out of my chair when I read the email. This feels pretty critical to Olivia and me.

STEPPING UP:

Man-made religion sometimes gets in the way of what God accepts. Isn't it great that God is open to all prayers? You and your family might want to start a listserve for people who would like to have a place to go with their less critical prayer requests. What an awesome ministry you could serve. In the meantime, you can pray as a family for your friends in need, and you can ask other believers you know to keep the people you know in their prayers.

LET'S TALK:

Lord of heaven and earth, thank you for hearing every prayer and treating each prayer as important. Also, thank you for making me aware of ways in which I can serve you and the people in my community. Amen.

DAY 25

Who Is That Crazy Person?

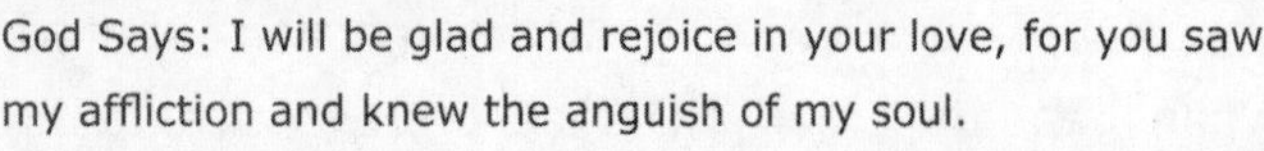

God Says: I will be glad and rejoice in your love, for you saw my affliction and knew the anguish of my soul.

Psalm 31:7

Lately my body is revolting. It's not like everyone I know isn't going through the same thing: our bodies are changing and we can't keep up. We're all dealing with periods and red angry zits that seem to make the announcement, "Watch out! Hormones in control!" And if the zits weren't embarrassing enough, I have to carry around pads and tampons that seem to fly out of my purse at the very worst possible minute. No wonder I feel nuts!

The thing is, I don't understand this crazy girl that shows up in my body for a week out of every month. One minute I'm happy, and the next minute I'm crying or yelling at someone. I see myself doing all these mean girl things, and I can't seem to stop myself. Not only do I feel like a nutcase, my body aches all over and I just want to lie in bed and watch movies.

So how do real women cope? I see my mom getting up and going to work. She takes care of our family. She even deals with clients without blowing up in their faces, the way I want to sometimes. My mom says it will get better. But every period has been worse than the last. I've talked with Melody and checked on the Internet, trying to find out how other girls handle this, but the suggestions were all over the place. I'm more confused now than I was when I started.

STEPPING UP:

The Internet offers information about many topics, even health issues. The problem is that unlike your mom or the doctor, the Internet does not know you or your family history. The information you find may not correspond with all of your symptoms. Whenever you have health problems, it's good to educate yourself. Moms, aunts, and older sisters are all a good resource. If you still are having health issues, a trip to your family doctor is always a good idea.

LET'S TALK:

God, when I'm confused, help me to turn to you and the trusted adults that you've put in my life. Help me to understand what's going on with my body and to find ways to cope with the changes I'm feeling. Give my family and friends the patience, love, and wisdom that I need when I'm that crazy girl. Amen.

DAY 26

Too Little, Too Much

God Says: Are they ashamed of their loathsome conduct? No, they have no shame at all; they do not even know how to blush.

Jeremiah 6:15

The girls in my P.E. class have had a great time making fun of me because I'm flat as a board. Seriously, it's so embarrassing. My mom finally gave in and took me to the lingerie department to look for some help. The lady there measured me and shook her head. After a few minutes she returned to my changing room with a huge pile of bras: double padded bras, water bras, jelly bras, and blow-up bras. I was so red I could have entered a tomato contest and won.

The sales lady kept saying that lots of people enhance their breasts with these bras. We must have been in that changing room for hours. Finally, when everyone agreed — everyone being four sales ladies and my mom — we left the store with three brand-new jelly bras. The next day when I was at school I started getting all these comments: they were like, "What happened to you? Did you take some kind of magic growth pill?" I'm not sure if being flat was worse than this.

Now tonight there is a quiz circulating through the school forum ranking girls in our class and their figures. My name is on there along with everyone else's.

Seriously, the comments next to my name make me want to puke. I can't believe people can be so mean. I wish I could crawl into a hole. Tomorrow I'm back to little ol' flat me. At least then I won't be trying to live up to other people's petty expectations.

STEPPING UP:

Internet quizzes and comment pages often lead to people feeling free to write mean things they would never say face-to-face. It's a coward's way of passing on their own insecurities. The only way these people can hurt you is if you take ownership of what they write about you. Don't give them the power. You know who you are. You're God's child.

LET'S TALK:

Lord, help me to stand tall and not change my looks just to fit in. Please don't let my classmates' pettiness get to me. Help me find true friends who believe in lifting each other up instead of tearing people down. Amen.

DAY 27

What Is My Purpose?

God Says: He who began a good work in you will carry it on to completion until the day of Christ Jesus.

Philippians 1:6

Our youth group leader, Miss Grace, asked us to blog or journal about why we think God created us. Like, what is our purpose? I keep looking at this question in bold print on my computer, and I don't have a clue. I can look at other people and see what God had in mind for them, but it just doesn't seem to be as clear for me.

Like Olivia, she's a great cook, and she's a super sister to Jack, Bill, and Maggie. I don't think I have one-tenth of her patience. And Chloe is, like, this fantastic artist, and she helps take great care of her grandmother who has Alzheimer's disease. Everyday when Chloe gets home, her grandma asks who she is. I think that would break my heart. Rachel is, like, only the most-beautiful, most-popular girl in the school. She takes time to talk to everyone no matter what group they're in. She makes everyone feel like they're cool. Then when I look at myself, I can only see what I'm not good at. Why is that?

Our youth leader says God had a plan for us before we were even born — I sure wish I could figure it out. He told us if we got stuck to ask someone what they think we do to make this world a better place. My fear is that if I ask someone, they'll tell me I'm just taking up space.

STEPPING UP: 

God gave every person his or her own unique talents and abilities. Think about the things you enjoy doing, like being a good listener. This allows you to be a trustworthy friend for someone in need. It's not just what you do better than someone else, but who you are that glorifies God.

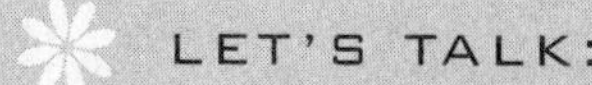

LET'S TALK:

Lord, it's hard to look at myself and see what you see. I want to live up to what you think I'm capable of doing. Lord, help me to claim my God-given talents and to perfect those skills so that I can share my gifts with others. Amen.

DAY 28

What's a Girl Supposed to Do?

God Says: Take note of this: Everyone should be quick to listen, slow to speak and slow to become angry, for man's anger does not bring about the righteous life that God desires.

James 1:19 – 20

Olivia and I have always been great friends. We like all the same things: horses, boys, chocolate malts, music, chatting online, skiing, football games, the pool, and lots more. We send PIX messages to each other every night to figure out what we're going to wear to school the next day. There isn't anything we don't discuss, from favorite T.V. shows to the gross stuff from health class.

The thing is, she's a total flirt. She's pretty quiet around other girls, but when the boys show up she gets all giggly and talks a million miles per hour. The boys circle around her, and the more she giggles at them the more they compete for her attention. She's tried to tell me she only gets that way because boys make her nervous. But I think she likes the attention.

Now don't get me wrong, it's not that I'm jealous. Yes, the

boys talk to me, but they ogle her like there isn't another girl for miles. Mostly, I just stand there, all fidgety. I try to get a word in edgewise but no one listens.

My sister told me that all that giggling will get old—with both Olivia and the boys. She said in the meantime to just enjoy Olivia's friendship while I have her here in town. I'm going to try to tell her that talking with the boys isn't half as important as making memories together.

STEPPING UP:

If you and your best friend are having trouble deciding where your priorities are when it comes to boys, you need to talk. Maybe you could come up with a signal that lets your friend tell you when you're feeling uncomfortable. Then you could head off to do something else you both enjoy.

LET'S TALK:

Heavenly Father, thanks for giving me confidence and a sense of humor. Help me to be sensitive to my friend's feelings. Also help me to realize the difference between lasting friendships and boy acquaintances. Amen.

DAY 29

Caretaker

God Says: I will demand an accounting from every animal. And from each man, too, I will demand an accounting for the life of his fellow man.

Genesis 9:5

That nasty woman who let the horses starve was in the news again today. I read about the trial on the net news. The story said she had animals taken away from her before. It also said that four of the twelve horses that were rescued had to be put down because they were too far gone.

What I don't get is why she was allowed to get more animals if she'd already had animals taken away. Don't they have family services for horses? This all seems so messed up.

It made me cry to read that article. I didn't realize any of the horses had died. When I get my emails with updates on Max, they just tell me about his progress. I know about Star and Socks because my friends get their emails and we forward them to each other. I was so wrapped up in "our" horses that I didn't think about what might happen to the other nine.

I wrote the rescue caretaker and asked what can be done so other people who hurt animals can't get more animals to abuse. The caretaker said that I should write my elected officials and tell them that I want to see stricter laws to protect the animals. He said even better than one letter would be a multitude of emails sent. He also suggested I get my friends to get their families to do the same.

STEPPING UP:

As a citizen, you have the right and the opportunity to write to your elected officials. The way to contact your government officials is to go to www.statelocalgov.net, then type in your state name. They will connect you to your government pages. Write a professional letter stating that you would like to see changes made to the laws concerning the ownership and care of animals. The more people who write, the more likely it is that the laws will change.

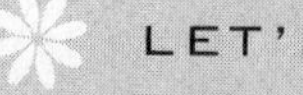

LET'S TALK:

Dear Father, thank you for letting me live in a country where even a kid's opinion can make a difference. Help me to be a strong voice calling for better care of your creation. When I stand before you, I want you to say, "Well done, good and faithful servant." Amen.

DAY 30

On Guard

God Says: Be on guard! Be alert!

Mark 13:33

So, I have this friend, Samantha. She IM'd me about this totally cool flirt site where girls don't have to pay to play. She said she's able to get on even though she isn't 18. Like, there was no ID check or anything.

Samantha was pumped about all these guys. They have to pay to use the site, and once they get on they answer ten multiple choice questions. Then Samantha rates their answers on a scale from 1 – 10. The guy with the highest score gets Samantha's email address and she gets his.

I messaged her back, saying "Are you for real? Now some guy you don't even know has your email address. What if this guy finds out you're in middle school? What if he's some nasty old pervert?"

She replied that I was just jealous and trying to ruin her fun.

Well, I backed off. But then I thought about how important Samantha is to me, and to God, so I decided to try one more time. Only this time I picked up my cell and called her directly.

I said, "Hey, I care about you, and I want you to be safe. What are you going to do when this guy finds out you're not 18? Not a great way to start a relationship. Besides, there are enough hot guys at our school to check out."

The next thing I know we are on the phone for, like, an hour talking about this really great basketball player, and then about what classes we'll have next quarter. By the time we got off the phone, we agreed it is better not to look for romance online while we're still in middle school.

STEPPING UP:

Tempting as boy-girl quizzes on the Internet are, they seldom lead to anything good. Never give your email address to anyone you don't know. If you've already done that, though, it's time to change your address immediately, before you get involved with a stranger.

LET'S TALK:

Lord, help me to make wise choices when I'm on the Internet. It's good to know that you're always with me, and I want to make you proud of everything I do. Help me to always talk honestly with my friends as we figure out the best way to live. Amen.

DAY 31

BFF?

God Says: Do not repay anyone evil for evil. Be careful to do what is right in the eyes of everybody. If it is possible, as far as it depends on you, live at peace with everyone.
Romans: 12:17 – 18

I've known Laura all my life. Our dads have worked together since I was four. Every summer our families would go to these cottages on Chippewa Lake. We'd hit the beach first thing in the morning, only coming in to eat. In the evenings we'd camp out under the stars, talking long into the night. Even though she's a year older, we were always really close.

A few days ago I ran into her at the ice rink, and she walked past me with her friends like I was invisible. I get that she's older and has older friends, but why can't we still be friends? We've been like vacation sisters.

So, I thought I'd give it one more try. I sent her an email telling her I understood about her friends, but that I missed her, and when she wasn't busy I'd love to hang out.

Then I got an IM from another friend telling me to read Laura's blog titled "STOP STALKING ME!"

I feel like I've been kicked in the stomach. The whole blog was about me stalking her, and how she's sick of having to put up with me. She wrote that I was some kind of charity case that her parents MADE her hang out with.

Who is this person, and what did she do with my friend Laura? I'm hurt. I'm mad. And most of all, I'm confused.

STEPPING UP:

It can really hurt when a friend pulls away. If you're in this situation, recognize that your friend may be going through something difficult. When you get a chance to talk to her, tell her you still think of her as a friend. But if she chooses to go on acting the way she is, then the privilege of your friendship will be withdrawn. In the meantime, do something to keep your mind off missing your friend. Go to the movies, paint a picture, or volunteer at a nursing home.

LET'S TALK:

Help me, Lord, to be understanding and forgiving when my friends hurt me. I know I never walk alone with you by my side. Help me to walk with others as lovingly and gently as you do. Amen.

DAY 32

Too Personal

God Says: Do nothing out of selfish ambition or vain conceit, but in humility consider others better than yourselves.
Philippians 2:3

Our school is having student council elections, and I'm running for sixth-grade class president. I've made posters that rock and banners listing events I'd like to see in school. I've spoken with the teachers and I've represented my take on things in the school debates. I've made a list of moneymaking ideas to support the changes I have in mind. I've sent emails to everyone I know asking for their votes. I've held a chat room. I wrote a whole election pitch and posted it on the school chat room.

I know I'm a good student. I care about people, and I like the whole political thing. I've done my homework. Most of the emails I've received have been positive — although I've gotten a few responses that haven't been so great like, "R U 4 real?" and "Get a life!" But I figure you have to be thick-skinned to be a politician. I'm hoping that my friends from cheer squad and student council will help me out. It would be so great to finally shine again.

The thing is, as much as I want to represent my classmates through student council I also like the idea that I will be class president. I know I shouldn't care about that, but it does feel good.

That is, it did feel good until I started getting emails and responses to my online campaign posts from someone I don't know. And the messages are gross. I should have known better than to post my email address in the chat room. Now being the center of attention doesn't feel so wonderful. Lord, I'm going to talk to my parents and let them know about my unknown emailer, and I'm going to change my email and blog address, just in case.

STEPPING UP: 

Putting your personal information on your blog or in chat rooms can lead strangers right to you. If you have already given out personal information, and now you're dealing with a stranger, you need to change your email and your blog address. Also make your parents aware that an unknown person is pursuing you. Then you can work out a plan of action together.

LET'S TALK:

Lord, it's so easy to think of the internet as just another way to talk to my friends. It scares me to think of all the dangerous people out there. Help me to learn how to be careful and how to honor you when I'm communicating online. Amen.

DAY 33

You're Going Out with Who?

God Says: Give your servant a discerning heart to govern your people and to distinguish between right and wrong.
1 Kings 3:9

My last crush was a total disaster — Olivia and I got in a big fight over her brother, who couldn't have cared less about me. Then Olivia and I didn't talk for days, and Jack still glares at me. After that terrible experience, I decided it was easier to leave love alone. That was until Friday evening. I never expected to meet Chase at the football game. We were just standing there waiting in the ticket line when we started talking.

Actually, he said something funny and I laughed. Chase said he liked my laugh. Then we talked for awhile, and even ended up walking around the track during the football game. We exchanged email addresses, and now we've emailed every night this week. It's so much easier to email than to talk on the phone. It gives me a chance to think. I'm not stumbling over myself saying something stupid.

Sometimes we IM for hours. I don't think I could have done that face-to-face in the beginning. I might have been too nervous. Now I feel like I've known Chase forever. I think I really like him. He says he really likes me ... I think this must be love. I think about him all the time and I can't wait to get to my computer every night. I get butterflies just thinking about talking to him. Lord, will you show me if this is real?

STEPPING UP:

If you're looking for a lasting relationship, then make a friend, not a boyfriend. Boyfriends come and go quicker than you can say, "Jesus loves me, this I know." Friends don't make your heart flip (totally overrated) or make you cry (thank goodness). Hanging out with a group of friends is so much easier and way less stressful.

LET'S TALK:

Dear Father, thank you when you send me someone who makes me feel special. Help me to keep my head on straight. Thanks for always being here to listen to me. Amen.

DAY 34

Stumbling

God says: Gossip separates close friends.

Proverbs 16:28

I majorly blew it today. Our church had this great harvest picnic this weekend. I wrote this funny story about my friend Rachel getting matched up in the three-legged race with the hottest basketball player in our youth group. I just didn't figure it was that big of a deal because I only emailed it to a couple friends who hadn't been at the picnic.

It was so funny at the time. Rachel drew a name for the three-legged race. Her eyes about popped out of her head when she read Mr. Hotstuff's name.

She's super short, like me. He's super tall. It was one of those unforgettable moments. There they were, stumble-running a three-legged race together — her short leg, his tall leg, and their mismatched legs! They stumbled, but before they'd reached the finish line they wiped out — arms and legs flying like a cartoon catfight. When the dust settled, I saw they had landed face-to-face, nose-to-nose, and nearly lips to lips. They quickly untangled themselves and then parted ways.

Later she confessed how her heart skipped a beat for a moment when they landed.

Well, there isn't a girl in our school who wouldn't have traded places with her.

But that doesn't matter because she's fuming. She emailed me MAD! MAD! MAD! I guess the email got forwarded to a lot more people than I ever intended. Now she's sure he'll find out how she feels, and she's out for blood.

I don't blame her. I put it out there for everyone to see. I guess it isn't any different than when Olivia asked about Jack and everyone knew how I felt. I guess I didn't learn much from that mess.

STEPPING UP:

Have you "shared" too much by giving out information about a friend that isn't yours to give? Tell your friend you're sorry you betrayed her trust. Tell her you realize it will take time for her to trust you again. Share with her that when you post information in the future, you'll always remember your friend's privacy. Finish by saying you value her friendship and that you'll work very hard at being a trustworthy friend—and then do it!

LET'S TALK:

Lord, I am not always a trustworthy friend, and I'm sorry. Help me to use good judgment when I'm speaking or writing, and help me to be the kind of friend you are. If I need to tell someone's business, I know I can always trust you. Amen.

DAY 35

Where I Ought to Be

God Says: All the days ordained for me were written in your book before one of them came to be.

Psalm 139:16

I cannot believe it! I won! I'm the sixth-grade class president. All day long people have been congratulating me in the halls. I belong. I have a place. I guess it's true — "When God closes one door, he opens another."

My mom was so excited for me when I called her with my good news. She said she would make my favorite meal of barbecue beef with mashed potatoes and corn soufflé to celebrate. Melody said she's really proud of me, and Dad left a text message saying, "Way 2 Go!" I feel so pumped!

I know if I had lost I would have been fine. Disappointed, but fine. Even though I've felt out of the loop since I didn't make the cheerleading squad, I have a purpose at school now. I can't wait to start implementing some of my ideas, like "Change a Life," where kids can throw their spare change in a jar after lunch and the money goes to purchasing a chicken or a goat for a family in Africa.

In the meantime, I want to find my opponent Josh and tell him he ran a good race. I know he wanted this office as much as I did. I want him to know I would still love to have him be involved in student council.

STEPPING UP:

Life is a lot like a coin. On one side you have wins; on the other you have losses. It is always good to keep both sides of the coin in clear view. It will help keep you humble and sensitive to others.

LET'S TALK:

Heavenly Father, help me remember that you always hold amazing opportunities for me and my future. Keep me humble when I hold positions of leadership, keep me sensitive to the needs of others, and keep your Word always in my mind. Amen.

DAY 36

Sleepless

God Says: Do not follow the crowd in doing wrong.

Exodus 23:2

Sleepovers have always been a blast at Brittany's — that is, until last night. After doing each other's nails and eating enough pizza and chocolate to make our faces break out for the next decade, we settled down to watch this ancient movie, "The Fog." We screamed at every scary scene, even though the ghosts were pretty lame. We laughed at each other for being such scaredy-cats.

Then Brittany decided we should do some scaring of our own. She got online and asked, "Who do we want to mess with?"

Emma suggested, "Trudy! She's a flirt."

"She thinks she's so hot!" said Samantha.

Brittany laughed. "Well, look who's online!" All the girls crowded around while Brittany chatted with Trudy like they were long-lost friends.

Everyone provided Brittany with suggestions. They just kept getting more and more personal.

It turned out the guy Trudy had a crush on had just started dating someone else, and Trudy needed a shoulder to cry on. Man, the girls ate up all the juicy details like candy. Trudy had no idea she was broadcasting her business to a room full of girls.

The more Brittany wrote, the more the girls whooped it up, and the more I felt sick to my stomach. I tried to tell them to stop, but then they got on my case, calling me "Goody Two-shoes." I backed off and didn't say anything.

Trudy's going to be the biggest joke at school on Monday. Now I can't even look myself in the mirror. I don't ever want to go to a sleepover again.

STEPPING UP: 

Face it. We girls can be vicious when we get together and settle on a target. Avoid situations where the environment is ripe for mean-girl syndrome. If you find yourself in the middle of a cyber-bullying situation, ask God for the strength to stand up against it. Cyber bullying is not okay.

LET'S TALK:

Lord, sometimes I find myself in situations with kids from school that make me feel like I have to go along with something I know is wrong. Please give me the strength to stand up for what is right. I always want to be an example of your love. Amen.

DAY 37 Caught Up In Gossip

God Says: A good name is more desirable than great riches; to be esteemed is better than silver or gold.

Proverbs 22:1

I was online looking up movie reviews when I saw my friend Samantha log on. I IM'd her and we started talking about all the drama going on in school. There's a new girl that all the boys are drooling over. She looks like she's straight from California, blonde hair, a nice tan, and clothes that rock. She walked right into our school, and everyone, and I mean everyone — teachers, the popular kids, the boys — started following her around like she's a movie star.

All of a sudden, who messages me but little Miss California. How did she get my screen name anyway? I reply and then tell Samantha that the new girl just starting chatting with me. She writes back, "No way!" and of course I write back, "Way!"

Miss California was asking me about school, and as I read Samantha was making fun of her chicken legs. So, I wrote back that little Miss California isn't all that cute anyway.

I added that I didn't see what all the fuss was about. Then I pressed the send button. All of a sudden I realized I had typed in the wrong box and sent the message straight to Miss California instead of Samantha.

Miss California immediately replied saying, "Well, I guess you and I aren't going to be friends."

Now I'm feeling terrible. I never gave her a chance. I can only imagine what she's thinking of me. I know what it feels like to be nailed by mean girls and here I went and jumped into the mean girl pool with both feet. I am so embarrassed. I feel awful, really, really awful.

I'm going to make some "I'm-sorry brownies" for Miss California. Maybe she'll give me a second chance at being a friend.

STEPPING UP:

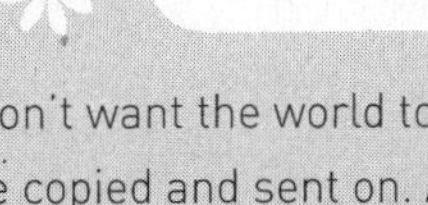

Never write something you don't want the world to read. Anything posted on the internet can be copied and sent on. Also, it's always important to think how you'd feel if someone else were writing something unkind about you. Do all you can to avoid gossiping. You'll feel much better about yourself.

LET'S TALK:

Lord, please forgive me when I gossip and spread rumors. Help me to be careful with the things I say, both out loud and online. I don't want to be one of the mean girls. Amen.

DAY 38

Get Informed

God Says: Be very careful, then, how you live—not as unwise but as wise.

Ephesians 5:15

My friend Rachel's older brother Ted loves music. He knows the words to almost every song ever recorded. He's started being asked by kids to DJ at their parties. The problem is that Ted and Rachel's family aren't wealthy, and all those songs for a DJ list can cost a fortune.

Ted started downloading songs from these supposedly free sites and trading songs with other kids online. At first it was just a few songs. Then Ted was, like, up all night long downloading songs. I heard Ted downloaded a couple thousand tunes. He even started making discs with requested songs for people. On Monday, the halls were buzzing with stories about Ted and his parents being sued by the Recording Association of America for unauthorized downloads. Rachel's family is totally freaking out. Turns out the recording industry has been tracking down people like Ted who were using peer-to-peer file sharing technology. Something like 11,000 people have been sued so far!

Because the computer is in his parent's name, they're being sued $4,000 to settle, or go to court and take a chance of being ordered to pay a huge amount for each and every song.

STEPPING UP:

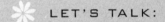

Music is protected by a copyright. This protects the musician's ownership of the songs. When a song is downloaded without permission, it's the same thing as stealing. The Record Association saw a huge drop in sales once people were able to download songs. That meant a loss of income for everyone associated with the song. So they started tracking down people. The safest way to download songs is to go to a reputable site where you pay to download the songs you're interested in.

LET'S TALK:

Lord, I love music and the musicians who produce it. They don't deserve to be cheated. Help me to remember those artists and all their hard work whenever I'm tempted by the ease and speed of file sharing. Amen.

DAY 39

Love Hurts!

God Says: I trust in the Lord. I will be glad and rejoice in your love, for you saw my affliction and knew the anguish of my soul.

Psalm 31:6-7

I haven't stopped crying for three hours. Chase and I broke up. We were together ... sort of ... for three whole weeks. It seemed like the real thing. Love, that is. We had awesome conversations and I thought about him every second of the day. I was so happy. I wouldn't have cared if it had been posted on every website, chat room, forum, IM, and email ever written.

I didn't care that I didn't get to see him every day because we talked for hours every night. He wrote me the coolest poems and sent me e-cards.

Then it happened. Olivia saw Chase at the mall holding hands with another girl. She took a cell phone picture and sent it to me. She said she wanted to make sure it wasn't him. But it was. They were walking, laughing, and holding hands, like I didn't exist. They were all over each other.

I don't ever want to fall in love again. It hurts too much. Melody has friends in high school who've had lots of long relationships, like for months, and when they break up it doesn't seem to bother them. They just move on to the next guy. I could never do that.

My sister, Melody, was totally cool. She spent the evening sharing all her break-up stories while we ate ice cream. I may have lost a guy I had a crush on, but the time with my sister was something I'll never forget.

STEPPING UP:

Emails and talking on the phone do not equal love. Think about 1 Corinthians 13. The description of true love doesn't include butterflies and forgetting about everything else. You will learn something from each relationship you're in — the importance of patience, kindness, honesty, and trust. Right now, focus on your family, school, and being the best friend you can be.

LET'S TALK:

Lord, help me to protect my heart. Thank you for showing me what real love is through your word, through my parents, and through your honest and true love. Amen.

DAY 40 No Tricks or Treats

God Says: For God said, "Honor your father and mother."
Matthew 15:4

Why do mothers always have to be right? Mom and I got into an argument because she wouldn't let me go trick-or-treating with my friends. Instead, she signed our family up for the Church Fall Foliage Night with hayrides and mazes. It sounded so lame to me compared to dressing up and running around with my friends.

Our church rented a farm for the evening. The night started with us going through the biggest hay maze I have ever seen. It was six feet tall and the size of a basketball court. They had apple bobbing and a barn rope where you could swing and drop into a hay mound. It was a blast! Even Mom and Dad tried the rope swing and dropped into the hay mound. They had a bonfire with cider, donuts, and marshmallows.

The hayride was sweet! Everyone was throwing hay, and then dad said, "Look! I've never seen so many stars." I haven't just looked and really seen the stars for a long time. They totally twinkle, just like in the song. Blake started pointing out the constellations and told us the bright star next to the moon was actually Jupiter, and that it wouldn't be this close again for twenty years.

The farmer heard us talking about the stars and said he had a telescope and asked if we wanted to have a look. It was amazing! You could see all the craters on the moon. He pointed out Jupiter and said it was fading, but Mars was gaining in brightness this month.

The night was anything but lame. I can't wait to check out more information about the night sky at the library. Until then I'm going to check and see what I can find online.

STEPPING UP:

Believe it or not, your parents always have your best interest in mind. As hard as it is to admit that your parents are doing a good job, your parents appreciate hearing it from you.

LET'S TALK:

Heavenly Father, thank you for time spent witnessing the glory of your creation. Help me to find the time to spend with my family appreciating the works of your hands. Amen.

DAY 41

Overwhelmed!

God Says: Never be lacking in zeal, but keep your spriritual fervor, serving the Lord.

Romans 12:11

I am fried. I don't think I even have a brain anymore. I've done so much homework my head feels like it's going to explode, and I still have piles more research to do. Our teacher wants us to use library research along with our online research. She must think we're college students or something! Has she forgotten that we still need to eat and sleep? When am I supposed to do my president's work for student council? I just want to tell her, "I have a life!"

My mother keeps telling me to stop griping and just get it done. I wish it were that easy. We went to the library together and I came home with a truckload of books. But there's so much information to wade through and so little time. Mom and I have been searching the internet trying to find things to fill in the gaps I have. We spent the whole night working.

LATER: I'm finally finished writing the paper. I've cited all my sources, and I've added a bibliography. Thanks goodness for my mom. I feel like crawling into bed and sleeping for the next week.

STEPPING UP:

Homework can be overwhelming. There are some great sites that are readily available on the net to assist you. Some of them are: www.schoolwork.org and www.Internetschoolhouse.com. But remember that information on the internet can change very quickly and cannot always be trusted. To check your facts, take a trip to the library and confirm your research in a scholarly book on the topic.

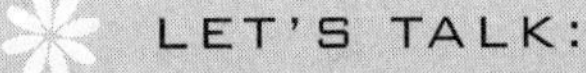

LET'S TALK:

Father, when I'm overwhelmed and feel like giving up, help me to focus and do my work with a clear head. Thank you for watching over every party of my life — even the homework! Amen.

DAY 42

Pay Up!

God Says: On the first day of every week, each one of you should set aside a sum of money in keeping with his income, saving it up, so that when I come no collections will have to be made.

1 Corinthians 16:2

All my friends have cell phones and they've had them practically since they were born.

Before my family decided to join the 21st century we all sat down to discuss the pros and cons of having a cell. Before we went to the cell phone store my parents made my sister and me sit down and sign a contract with them. We had to agree when and how we would use our cell phones. We also agreed to pay them a portion of the cell phone bill. Dad and Mom say it will teach us responsibility.

Even with all that, I still totally love my cell. Last week Samantha had a crystal party. We brought our cells and we decorated them with this special glue and jewels. Mine looks so sweet. It's pink with purple and magenta crystals. The only problem is that I've spent all my money on the carry case and jewels. I got so engrossed in all the glitziness that I didn't stop even when I knew I was running through all my cash.

My parents are expecting me to pay my portion of the cel bill tomorrow. Now I have to tell them that I spent my mone decorating my cell. My contract with my parents says if I don pay them, I have to give up my phone until I can. I won't have any more money until I babysit this week. I'll think twice about spending money the next time I need to pay my bill.

STEPPING UP: 

Having a job, money, and responsibilities are all part of life. It takes time to learn how to balance all three. Sometimes money lessons can be painful. The great thing is, learning this lesson early on in life will make managing money as an adult WAY easier!

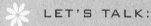

LET'S TALK:

Heavenly Father, help me to be responsible so that I don't have trouble managing money. Thank you for helping me learn to be a good steward of my resources. Amen.

Cheater!

God Says: For there is nothing hidden that will not be disclosed, and nothing concealed that will not be known or brought out into the open.

Luke 8:17

I've been studying all week for a pre-algebra test. I've been eating, sleeping, and breathing math. I'm always at a total loss with anything using numbers. So my parents got me a tutor. She's really helped me break things down to small bites. For the first time ever I went into the class feeling confident about a math test.

I plugged through that test slow and steady, problem by problem. I was feeling really good about my work. Then I noticed the girl across from me text messaging. I went back to my work. But then I saw her checking her cell and writing an answer on her test. She was cheating! She saw me and turned her back toward me.

I'm fuming. I studied, and I'll be lucky to get a B. This girl cheats using her cell phone, and she'll get an A. What do I do with that information? If I tell, I'm a snitch. If I don't tell, she'll get away with a good grade that she doesn't deserve. I wish I'd never seen her. Now I'm stuck knowing too much.

I'm thinking a possible solution could be that I drop an anonymous note in the school suggestion box. The note won't point fingers at anyone, but will make the teachers aware that they need to rethink cell phones being allowed in class during tests.

STEPPING UP: 

If you're an honest student, cheating is a very hard thing to accept. It's even more difficult to put up with when you've had to work so hard to get a passing grade.

Take pride in your effort and accomplishment. You know you earned your grade. If you feel comfortable, talk to your teacher about what you saw and leave the decision in his or her hands.

 LET'S TALK:

Lord, I know you see all things. Help me and my classmates not to be tempted to take the easy way out by cheating. Help me not to judge others, but to always seek to understand. Amen.

DAY 44

You're Not the Boss of Me!

God Says: Each of you should look not only to your own interests, but also to the interests of others.

Philippians 2:4

Youth group yesterday totally rocked. Olivia and I were chosen to head up our church service plan for our community. Every year we choose a service project for six Saturdays through the school year. We raise funds at church for whatever supplies we'll need. We also contact businesses that might be willing to partner with us. Our parents and associate businesses work on the project together with us.

Last year the students cleaned up the city park and planted flower boxes. The year before the kids and parents built a playground in one of the poor neighborhoods.

The part I'm not so excited about, though, is that all of a sudden Olivia is acting like she's the BOSS OF EVERYTHING!

We've always worked great as a team, but not this time. She's taken this whole project on as "Olivia's Last Stand" before she moves. Within minutes she was on the Internet looking up Habitat for Humanity, saying we're going to outdo every project ever done by our church. Now don't get me wrong. I think Habitat for Humanity is a great cause, but we didn't even discuss it. She's already telling everyone how it's going to be without letting us discuss our options, or vote, or anything. Someone needs to tame the beast, and everyone says it should be me. I'm calling Olivia and asking her over to make some cookies for our planning committee. Heavy discussions always work better with cookies and milk.

STEPPING UP: 

Group projects can be totally fun, as well as a great opportunity to learn about leadership. Remember that everyone in the group needs to be involved and contributing to the decisions, and you'll be amazed at what you can accomplish together!

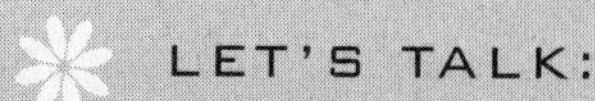

LET'S TALK:

Dear Father, help me to remember the importance of everyone's involvement in major decisions. When I need to have tough conversations with my friends, show me how to speak in love and understanding. Amen.

DAY 45

Personal Banker

God Says: Dishonest money dwindles away, but he who gathers money little by little makes it grow.

Proverbs 13:11

I usually have at least a little spending money. Mrs. Wiard has me babysit her son every other Friday and on Saturdays until she gets home from work. My parents say I'm supposed to put half of the money I earn into savings. I give a portion of my earnings to church, and I pay for part of my cell bill. After I take care of my responsibilities I usually have a few dollars left over to spend on whatever I want.

Rachel asks to borrow money almost every day. She says she forgot her lunch money, or she needs to pay for a library book fine, or she owes money for a field trip. Every day the reason is different, but it all adds up to the same thing. She has her hand open and acts like I'm her personal bank. Now, I understand her family isn't rolling in dough, but neither is mine. I earn my money, and I don't want to just give it away like that.

At first, Rachel said she was going to pay me back. But she never did. I mentioned it once or twice, and she got all weird on me, like I was Scrooge counting my change. The only thing that changed after that was Rachel stopped offering to pay me back. I know the next time she asks I should say no. But I don't want her or my friends to think I'm stingy. Why does money have to be such a pain? First I had to give up my cell phone for 10 days until I could pay my overdue bill, and now I feel like I'm giving all my money to support Rachel's money issues.

So I prayed about it and I came up with a great idea. I'm going to help Rachel find a job so she can have her own money to spend.

STEPPING UP:

Lending money is always a stress on a relationship. If you lend money, realize you may never see it again. Remember all the work that went into earning your money. You can take pride in that work, and while it's always good to help out a friend in need you shouldn't let anyone take advantage of your generosity.

LET'S TALK:

Lord, help me to find the strength to stand up for myself so that I'm not being taken advantage of. Also, please help me to be a good example of what a positive work ethic is all about. Thanks, God. Amen.

DAY 46

Party On!

God Says: If you do what is right, will you not be accepted? But if you do not do what is right, sin is crouching at your door; it desires to have you, but you must master it.

Genesis 4:7

I just got this email inviting me to a Friday after-school party at Blake's house. His parents both work really long hours, and a lot of kids have started hanging out at his place. It's become the place to be. There's always a lot of music and games, like pizza-eating contests.

I do have to say at first I was pumped that I was asked. It's not like I could go or anything. I have to babysit. But I'd love to be able to hang out with Blake and my other friends at a cool party. I started thinking about how I could get out of work so I could go. I pictured myself all glammed up, being part of this great party.

But then I realized Mrs. Wiard would have to leave work early if I went, and I know she needs the money. And if Mrs. Wiard ever found out I lied to her, she would fire me.

Besides, I don't think I could handle the disappointment on my parents' faces, especially after the whole cell phone thing.

Yep, I'm thinking God wouldn't be proud of me either. I emailed my response: "Thanks, but no thanks."

STEPPING UP:

Trust takes a lifetime to build and only seconds to destroy. Losers are people who grab that momentary pleasure and tell that little lie. They don't think through to the consequences of their actions. Adults are people who take on responsibility and follow through, even when it's hard. Welcome to the club!

LET'S TALK:

Dear Father, thanks for guiding me to make good choices. Sometimes I get caught up in the whole draw of being cool. But it's even more important that I'm cool with you and with who I am. Thanks for keeping me focused on the big picture. Amen.

DAY 47

Check the Schedule

God Says: Teach us to number our days aright, that we may gain a heart of wisdom.

Psalm 90:12

I've got so many things going on — school, youth group, tumbling class, service hours, working on student council as class president, babysitting, homework, football games, hanging out with my friends, and chatting online. I was beginning to get things mixed up. My mom suggested we run to the store and buy a planner.

We had a really good talk along the way about managing time. Mom shared how she gets up in the morning before anyone else just so she can have quiet time to read the Bible and pray. She told me she prays for Dad, Melody, and me every morning. She said she's started every day with the Word since she gave her heart to the Lord when she was fourteen. Her Sunday-school teacher challenged each of her classmates to read the Word every morning before school for three months. Mom said she found her days went much better when she started her day with God.

Anyway, it feels good to have everything reasonably written down by the day and even by the hour! I was looking at my calendar, feeling pretty good about my new life starting with time in the Word in the morning and ending with time talking with God here on my blog.

STEPPING UP: 

All the different activities in our hectic lives can be consuming. You need to make a conscious effort to take control. It requires reevaluating your responsibilities and priorities. Once you have done that, you can reschedule accordingly, putting Christ first.

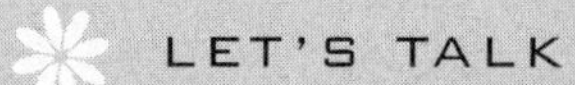

LET'S TALK:

Thank you, God, for scheduling me in every moment of every day. Your love is so amazing. Lord, help me to change my focus from the day-to-day stuff to remembering you first. I want you to be the first and last thing I think of everyday. Amen.

DAY 48

Art or Mutilation?

God Says: The way of a fool seems right to him, but a wise man listens to advice.

Proverbs 12:15

Everyone in middle school — I mean everyone — has pierced ears. A lot of my friends have more than one set of piercings for earrings. Melody told me that some kids at the high school have other piercings, like in their eyebrows or their belly buttons. There's a girl at the burger shop with her tongue pierced. We love to have her wait on us so we can watch her talk with that silver ball bouncing around.

My parents are totally against me getting my ears pierced, and I don't get what the big deal is. They're so stuck in the last century. No piercings, and don't even talk about body art! According to my parents, tattoos are a mutilation of my body's temple.

I told my parents I'm not going to go crazy and pierce every extremity of my body. I just want to get my ears pierced. It's not like I'm asking to get body art from head to toe or anything. I only want two little matching holes in my ears so I can wear earrings like everyone else.

I'm going to do some research on doctors who provide piercing services, and then I'm going to talk to my parents. I hope my parents and I can get to a place we can both agree on.

STEPPING UP:

Being obedient to your parents when they seem to be so last century can really be a drag. Have you asked your parents what their real concern is? When they won't allow you to do what "everybody else is doing," you can be certain that they have a good reason for it. Honest, open dialogue is the best way to prevent misunderstandings and arguments.

LET'S TALK:

Dear Father, I know you tell us to obey our parents. And I want to be a good kid. I feel like I'm growing up and should be able to determine how I dress and act. But Lord, I will accept what they say. Thank you, God, for helping me listen to you and my parents. Amen.

DAY 49

Food, Glorious Food!

God Says: "Everything is permissible"—but not everything is beneficial ... So whether you eat or drink or whatever you do, do it all for the glory of God.
1 Corinthians 10: 23, 31

I love food. I love every kind of food. Regular American food, Chinese food, Mexican food, Italian food, junk food, health food, vegetables, meat, potatoes, fruit, bread, pasta, chocolate, and ice cream. I've always been able to eat what I want and not worry about it. Now don't get me wrong. I'm not a binger, who sits and eats a whole bag of chips at a time. But I like to sit down and eat a salad, spaghetti and meatballs with some garlic bread, and, of course, some lemon ice for dessert. YUM!

Now all of a sudden, I'm starting to gain weight. I'm not eating anything differently ... except for maybe sleepovers, where we eat our way through the night. Mom says it's probably just a stage and not to worry. But I am worried. I don't want to get too heavy.

So I talked to the girls the other night at the sleepover, and Trudy said she'll go a whole day not eating after a slumber party. And Brittany said she tried her mother's diet pills, but they made her feel crazy anxious.

I couldn't believe my ears. None of these girl's answers sounded healthy or good to me. Olivia, Samantha, Rachel, and I were totally blown away. We decided we were going to find a better way to keep to a healthy weight.

STEPPING UP:

Most Americans have forgotten how to eat the way God meant for us to eat. He made our bodies to use food as a fuel. We've gotten lazy and eat packaged foods with too many bad ingredients. And our jumbo portions are jumbo sizing us.

The healthy answer to the changes in your body is to eat the way God planned. Eat smaller portions. Whenever possible, enjoy foods the way God made them — fruits, vegetables, dairy products, fish, meat, and grains. An occasional treat is fine, but be sensible and avoid fad diets and quick-fixes.

Also remember that your body is going through a ton of changes right now, and one of those changes is that you'll add on some pounds, especially in your hips. This is normal and healthy, and all part of becoming a woman.

LET'S TALK:

Lord, sometimes I feel horrible about my body. I look in the mirror and wonder how anyone could think I'm beautiful. Help me to see myself as your daughter, created in your image to glorify you. Amen.

DAY 50

Dress Code Kills Freedom of Expression

God Says: In everything set them an example by doing what is good. In your teaching show integrity, seriousness and soundness of speech that cannot be condemned.
Titus 2:7 – 8

Our principal had a total meltdown! This morning in assembly she announced that next Monday we're going to start a new school dress code. We are no longer allowed to wear sleeveless shirts, shirts with sayings, or hats. Boys are not to wear earrings. Girls are only allowed to have one set of stud earrings. Any other piercings are to be covered. There're not to be any stomachs showing. No oversized pants that hang down below the waist. Everyone is to wear dark pants and white or light-colored tops without any wild designs. I can't believe this is happening! I'm the class president — why didn't she discuss this with me or the other student council members before she made the decision?

She says it's because the kids in school are not being respectful of each other. She gave this whole talk on how the clothes we have been wearing are distracting us from the learning process. "Learning is a business," she said, "and you should dress like you're going to a job." She must not watch the Morning Show. They just did a whole fashion show for the winter line, but it sure didn't include any of our principal's fashion choices. I feel like I'm going to a prison. Doesn't it say somewhere in the Constitution that we have the freedom of expression?

Maybe as class president I can have student council start a petition. I might be able to get the principal to let us have a school vote. There has to be something we can do.

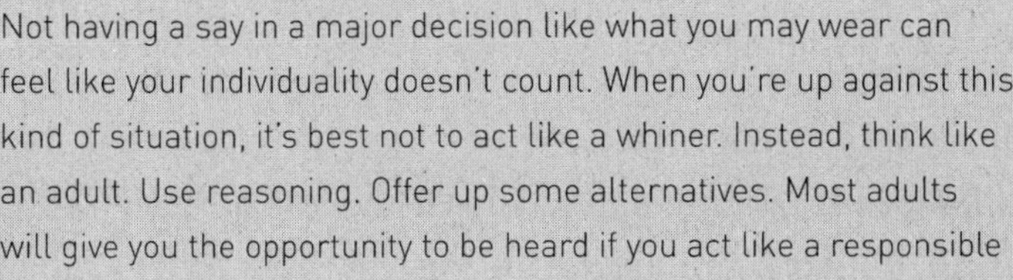

STEPPING UP:

Not having a say in a major decision like what you may wear can feel like your individuality doesn't count. When you're up against this kind of situation, it's best not to act like a whiner. Instead, think like an adult. Use reasoning. Offer up some alternatives. Most adults will give you the opportunity to be heard if you act like a responsible person.

LET'S TALK:

Dear God, thank you for making me my own person. I love being an individual, with my own unique talents and gifts. Thank you that there's only one me in the world! Help me to find ways to express my individuality while glorifying you. Amen.

DAY 51

Blah! Blah! Blah!

God Says: Each one should test his own actions. Then he can take pride in himself, without comparing himself to somebody else.

Galatians 6:4

There's this new girl at school, Michelle, who sits with us at lunch. We didn't start off so well when she moved here from California, but now we get along great. The problem is she talks more than all of us together. Every other word is I, I, I.

Still, she's really funny and nice. Being from California she has this whole unique take on life. When she gets on a roll, it's nonstop talking about problems, the guy she had a crush on in California, her soccer team, her hair, her pain-in-the-neck brother. I just want her to come up for a breath so we can hear someone else's voice for a few minutes. Rachel, Olivia, Samantha, and I hardly ever get a chance to talk with each other during lunch anymore.

The rest of us want to be good listeners, but how much can you listen to? It just would be nice to get a word in edgewise. I've tried to jump in on the few occasions when she does pause for drama, but she acts like no one else has spoken, and then she revs back up again.

How do you tell a new friend she needs to take a break and let other people sitting at the table have a chance to speak? I don't want to be rude. I just want her to realize she isn't the only one with a life.

I'm thinking of suggesting that we have a potluck at lunch. This is something like what we do in student council, where we all get to share ideas and suggestions. The potluck is that everyone gets to share one juicy detail of what is going on in her life. That way everyone gets a chance to talk and listen.

STEPPING UP: 

Some people talk because they need attention. Others talk because they're nervous. God gave us one mouth and two ears for a reason. He wants us to listen twice as much as we talk.

 LET'S TALK:

Dear Father, thank you for good friends and for the opportunities to listen to and learn from them. Help me to recognize situations in which people need me to listen, just as you always listen to me. Amen.

DAY 52

Clean It Up!

God Says: Nor should there be obscenity, foolish talk or coarse joking, which are out of place, but rather thanksgiving. Ephesians 5:4

My friends and I have been sending email jokes to each other for a long time. They're all pretty lame, but I think that's why they're funny. I have to say that we've gotten some pretty classic ones.

What did the hotdog say when he reached the finish line?
I'm a wiener! I'm a wiener!!

Why did the child eat his homework?
Because it was a piece of cake.

Why did the computer cross the road?
To get a byte to eat.

We all try to top each other's jokes. Not long ago we started rating the jokes. Blake comes up with the funniest ones. He says he goes to the kids' jokes website to find most of them. He's also on some kind of joke-a-day list. I've come to look forward to reading the jokes first when I check my email.

But lately some of the jokes aren't so funny. Several people have been posting jokes that are pretty crude. I don't want to sound like a Goody Two-shoes, but I really am offended by some of the dirty words. I don't know why people can't just keep it good, clean fun. Why does everything always seem to start out fun and then go down the tubes? The funny thing about the jokes is that they aren't so funny anymore. I know my parents wouldn't laugh if I told those jokes at the dinner table. I'm going to post a bunch of clean jokes and see if I can get our email group back on the right path.

STEPPING UP:

It can be pretty disappointing when an activity you love and appreciate goes sour. If you can't change these situations, it's best to drop them completely. The internet is full of offensive material that doesn't bring glory to the Lord. The foul language and images that you might come across have no place in your mind.

LET'S TALK:

Dear God, I love that you gave humans a sense of humor. It always feels so good to laugh. Help me to find humor in the appropriate places. Give me the courage to stand up for what I know is respectable. Amen.

DAY 53

Gone

God Says: For God so loved the world that he gave his one and only Son, that whoever believes in him shall not perish but have eternal life.

John 3:16

I am heartbroken. Mrs. Walker, a woman from church, was killed in a car accident this weekend. She was returning from a weekend visiting her son in college. Mrs. Walker was always a really upbeat person. She would bring these really yummy treats to youth group every week. I especially loved her homemade carrot cake bars. Now she's dead. How can that be? I just saw her in the hall on Thursday night when I went to youth group. She was so pumped about going to see her son.

I heard her sister flew in and is with her son trying to get the funeral together. I feel so bad for them. I wish I knew what to do to help.

I just can't believe she is gone. Not gone for a day or a week or a month. She is gone. It just seems so very, very wrong. She had a whole life ahead of her.

I realize people die every day. I just never thought it would be someone I knew. I can't imagine going to youth group and not seeing her there. It's never going to be the same.

I've had all these weird thoughts, like if she can die so can I, or what keeps my parents from getting killed on the road? What keeps any of us from dropping dead this very moment?

I'm trying to keep in mind that everything passes though God's hands, but sometimes it's so hard to understand why things happen the way they do.

STEPPING UP:

Death is a painful experience for the survivors. The sense of loss can be overwhelming. God made us to be born and live in the world, and then, when we die, to be brought into his presence and glory. It's right and good to mourn when a person passes away, but we can rest in the knowledge of God's everlasting life and love.

LETS TALK:

My loving Father, I ask for your peace and your presence in every part of my life. In the times of confusion and pain, remind me of your eternal love and help me to rest in you. Amen.

DAY 54

Out of Words

God Says: But love your enemies, do good to them... Then your reward will be great.

Luke 6:35

Ever since I didn't make the cheerleading squad, Emma has been going out of her way to make me feel like a loser. I can walk in with a sweet new outfit, and she'll take one look at me and say something like, "What online reject store did you order that from?"

Of course I want to defend myself, but I can't. If there were a class in snappy comebacks I'd get a big fat F. So I just stand there feeling stupid and then stew about it for the rest of the day. Part of me wants to come up with a zinger of my own, and then I remember that isn't what Jesus would want me to do.

The other bad thing about Emma is that after her attention is off me, she moves on to the next victim. I can't believe she has turned into such a mean girl. I used to think of her as a really good friend. And what surprises me even more is the fact that about half of the squad is right there backing up her meanness.

Emma is on the attack a lot, but she does have levels. The

girls in her circle are Level One. They only get bashed if she's gone too long without a fresh victim. She can't afford to alienate her groupies, even if all they do is laugh at what she says. They give her power. Level Two are kids like me that make good targets because we don't snap back. She's mean to us, but not nearly as mean as she is to the third level. Level Three victims are girls who stammer, cry, or turn red when she attacks.

In the future I'm going to try to stop Emma in her tracks with a comment like "I hope you start feeling better. Personally, I'm feeling really great," and then walk away. Maybe by my example, they'll find a better way to treat people.

STEPPING UP:

There's a little bit of Emma in most of us, isn't there?
We look at someone and think they walk funny or their hair is weird. We can find any number of other things to laugh about. But making fun of people isn't a laughing matter. Focusing on someone else's faults instead of dealing with our own might seem like fun at the time, but it puts us in the same category as the mean girls. This keeps us from growing into the strong confident women we were born to be.
Take a step up. Compliment people instead of cutting them down. See if you don't feel much better about yourself and others.

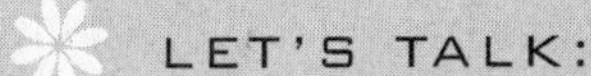

LET'S TALK:

Dear God, you are Love, Kindness, and Acceptance.
When I take those qualities and claim them as my own, I feel better about myself, and I can pass your love along to others. Amen.

DAY 55

Saying Goodbye

God Says: The Lord your God goes with you; he will never leave you nor forsake you.

Deuteronomy 31:6

Olivia's house finally sold last week, and we've had to say good-bye. I didn't think it would hurt as much as it did. I helped her pack up her room, putting all her favorite books into boxes and packing all her clothes into suitcases. It took us a long time to pack because we kept uncovering old memories. Her scrapbooks and photo albums are full of pictures of the two of us giggling at the lake or the park. Her CD collection has albums from artists that we saw in concert together. Her closet was full of outfits that we'd shared — I left with a pile of sweatshirts and t-shirts that she'd borrowed. Everything had a memory attached to it, and it was so hard to see those memories stuffed into boxes. At one point I just grabbed a stuffed animal and sobbed.

Mom, Dad, and Melody came over to see them off. Mom gave them a basket full of snacks for the road, and then we all stood in a circle and held hands while Dad prayed for their safety during the trip and blessings in their new home. Then they got in the car and drove away, the moving van following behind. We all stood and waved until we couldn't see them anymore.

Mom keeps telling me that it will be easy to stay in touch online and on the phone, and maybe Olivia will be able to come back for a visit at Christmas or next summer. But it won't be the same at all. No more Olivia to giggle with, or sing funny songs with, or just be best friends with. Lord, what will I do without her?

STEPPING UP: 

All of us will experience some sort of loss in our lives, and it never gets any easier. It's hard to imagine how life will go on after such a huge change, but in those dark times remember that the Lord is near, and he will never leave you.

LET'S TALK:

Dear Lord, keep me close when I go through dark days. I praise you that you are unchanging, and that I can always run to you when I'm lonely. Amen.

Mystery Card

God Says: Let him not deceive himself by trusting what is worthless, for he will get nothing in return.

Job 15:31

I got another email card this morning. The first card was simple. Just a bird saying how "tweet" it was to see me every day. Signed, a friend. The second card said, "B4 I knew U my days were PU, now I can't W8 2 B with U! C U N class!" Everyday the cards got sweeter and sweeter until I had a grand total of seven.

This afternoon I finally got up the nerve to talk to Kevin, this guy in my English class. I was positive he was the one sending the cards. I mean, it didn't take a rocket scientist to figure it out, since they all had his email address on them. So I went up to him in the hall and started gushing about how romantic it was and how I'd jump out of bed each morning to read my email. I told him I felt like I was floating after reading his message.

There was just one problem. While I was doing all this gushing, I failed to watch his face. It wasn't until I turned off the geyser that it hit me — he had no clue! He stammered something about somebody using his email to make his life miserable. He apologized and said he was going to change his email address.

How could they be so cruel? I'm embarrassed and hurt. I really liked getting those cards and feeling special to someone. I'm angry at whoever pulled this mean trick on both of us. What did they have to gain by playing with our email information and my heart?

STEPPING UP: 

Any time you share your password with your friends, you take a chance that your email can be used by someone else. Your best friend may not use it to cause you trouble, but someone they know may pick up the information from your friend and run with it. If you let your information slip, change your password as quickly as possible. Also, never use passwords that can easily be figured out, like your name, your address, or even your dog's name. People take pleasure in seeing if they can break your "code."

LET'S TALK:

Lord, I guess some people must really be bored if they find joy at someone else's expense. Or maybe they do mean things because it makes them feel powerful. Either way, I can't help but feel sorry for them. I also feel sorry for their targets. I lift them all up to you, Lord. Heal their hurting places. Take the meanness out of them, and fill them with your love. Amen.

DAY 57 Exaggerate This!

God Says: Show me your ways, O Lord, teach me your paths; guide me in your truth and teach me, for you are God my Savior, and my hope is in you all day long.

Psalm 25:4 – 5

Lately I've been having a hard time trusting my friend Trudy. She has this way of exaggerating things — well, pretty much everything. If she searched on the Internet for five minutes, she says she's been on the Internet for hours. If she buys an outfit, it's either more expensive or less expensive, depending on if she wants you to think that she got the best buy or the best designer outfit. If she's late, she creates a story so elaborate it could rival any fairytale.

So, I have found myself doubting everything she says. I'm not sure how much to believe and how much to chalk up to her way of exaggerating. Her reputation as a storyteller has really put off a lot of people at school.

The other day a couple of girls confronted her, and she really did some fast talking trying to save face. I could see she was squirming, and I sort of felt sorry for her. But on the other hand, I think she needs to face up to the facts and stop living a life of fiction. I just hate to see her called out in front of a lunchroom full of people.

I am not sure how to try to save her from herself. I know you, God, can't be happy to hear all her half-truths. I'm thinking I could ask Trudy over and we could talk. Maybe if I tell her that she's great without all the extras and people just want to get to know her she won't feel the need to exceed.

STEPPING UP:

People who exaggerate need attention. They think that if they make their lives more interesting, people will want to be their friends. The reality is that because of their half-truths, people begin to doubt them and pull away.

If you confront someone about exaggerating, it's best to do it in private. Tell the person that you care about her. Let the person know that she doesn't need to stretch her stories to have people like her. She is likable enough without all the extra information.

LET'S TALK:

Dear God, help me to always follow Christ's example by telling the absolute truth, without any false details. I am complete in you, just as you made me! Amen.

DAY 58

Comfort

God Says: Praise be to the God and Father of our Lord Jesus Christ, the Father of compassion and the God of all comfort, who comforts us in all our troubles, so we can comfort those in any trouble with the comfort we ourselves have received from God.

2 Corinthians 1:3 – 4

I guess it's true about everything — even bad things — happening for a reason. Olivia and her family have finally moved away, and I miss her more than I could have imagined. Thankfully we can still keep in touch online. She IM'd me late last night, telling me she'd been crying all night because a guy she liked dumped her. It was like an instant replay of me and Chase. When she started her new school he swept her off her feet. They talked all the time, and when they weren't talking they were IMing. He sent her e-cards and dedicated songs to her. They liked each other for three whole weeks, just like me and Chase. Then all of a sudden, she sees him walking down the hall holding another girl's books. The worst part was that he announced their breakup right there in the hall with hundreds of people watching. At least I didn't have to go through that embarrassment.

Anyway, the deal is that I could totally relate. I told her that I had gone through the same thing. I thought I knew Chase. I thought we'd be together forever. I thought I was in love. Then I realized that the love I had for him was really a crush. I also realized it's much better to have friends — as in plural — as in girls and boys — to hang out with. There aren't the butterfly highs or, thankfully, the pillow-soaked lows. Just friends, getting together, having a good time.

She IM'd me saying, "Thanks for listening and understanding. I'm going to give up boyfriends and stick to friends." So I guess I needed to do all that hurting so I could comfort a friend.

STEPPING UP: 

Being a good listener is one of the greatest gifts you can give as a friend. Sharing a similar hurt without making it all about you is a way to say you understand your friend's pain. Learning from your past hurts is a gift to you.

LET'S TALK:

Dear Father, help me to remember that you can use every experience, good as well as bad, for your perfect purpose! Help me to learn from the difficult times in my life so that I can be a better friend to those in need. Amen.

DAY 59

I'm Not My Sister!

God Says: But now, this is what the Lord says—he who created you, O Jacob, he who formed you, O Israel: "Fear not, for I have redeemed you; I have summoned you by name; you are mine."

Isaiah 43:1

We were at my aunt and uncle's house tonight, and I am so ARRGH!

My uncle is forever calling me by my sister's name. Tonight when he hugged me hello he said, "Hi, Melody." I corrected his mistake and he said, "I'm sorry. I know it's you. It's just that you look so much like your sister."

Like, that's supposed to make me feel better? What am I? Chopped liver? I just don't get it. Are uncles supposed to have favorites? He obviously thinks my sister hung the moon and I'm not that important.

The bad thing is that it makes me feel mad at Melody. I don't want to talk to her or even look at her. I have to remind myself she didn't do anything. It's my uncle who really upset me. Then I get even more upset with myself because he's my uncle. Family is important, and I shouldn't let a little thing like my uncle mixing up our names bother me so much.

I thought about asking Mom and Dad if I could skip out on trips to their house in the future, but how long can you avoid a relative? And quite honestly, when I'm not getting called by the wrong name, my uncle can be pretty cool. Not long ago we went to the zoo, and my uncle showed us how God made each animal just as it needed to be to survive.

So I guess I just need to do something memorable. Next week I'm going to talk to my uncle. I'm going to tell him I appreciate him for the individual he is and to tell him about the individual I am.

STEPPING UP:

Being compared to someone else can be disheartening, especially when it's obvious the other person is favored.
Remember that you are a unique individual made by the creator of the universe! Focus on your own talents and accomplishments, and know how deeply you are loved.

LET'S TALK:

Dear Father, I know you know each one of us as the individuals you created. I also know you want us to love one another as you love us. Sometimes the whole comparison thing can be tough. Help me not to be resentful, but to love and forgive as you forgive me. Amen.

DAY 60

My Shirt!

God Says: The man with two tunics should share with him who has none, and the one who has food should do the same.

Luke 3:11

Rachel emailed me asking to borrow my blue shirt. When I went looking for it, my shirt was missing.

Melody and I wear the same size. I used to think that this was a good thing because we could have double the wardrobe. How cool is that? With double the wardrobe we could go more days without wearing the same things to class. We could mix and match so many clothes it would feel like we had a celebrity closet!

All of this was great in concept, but turned out to be a total nightmare in reality. Now I can never find my stuff. I look for my jacket and find it in the dirty clothes hamper. The last time I went looking for my favorite jeans, I found them in the back of her closet wadded up in a ball. My favorite shirt had a red stain of unknown origin on it. Melody says it wasn't her, but I know for a fact it wasn't me. Unless we have another mystery sister hiding in the attic, one of us has a poor memory. Besides, I keep my clothes neatly hung and color coordinated. Her closet looks like a hamster nest—and that's on a good day.

Mom suggested that we work out a list of rules. Melody's solution was that we should have some favorite clothes marked "HANDS OFF" and that we just share the remainder of our stuff.

STEPPING UP:

Sharing is a challenge in every family. It's one of the civilized behaviors taught in a child's development, but it's never easy, especially when the person you're sharing with doesn't have the same respect that you do for the item. Having rules you can agree on before you get into a situation can help avoid problems. An example could be: Items being borrowed must be returned the next day in the same condition, clean and ready for the next use. If this rule is not followed, then the borrower loses the privilege to borrow again.

LET'S TALK:

God, I know you want us to be able to share our things with other people. Believe me, I don't want to care about stuff more than I care about the people I love. But I also think you want us to take care of the gifts you allow us to have.

Help me to be fair and teach me how to be a good example. I want to please you, Lord. Amen.

DAY 61

Something's Missing

God Says: Turn to me and be gracious to me, for I am lonely and afflicted.

Psalm 25:16

I'm feeling so lonely tonight, and I'm really not sure why. I was at school all day, surrounded by people I know. Then I rode the bus home. And I've been online chatting with more friends ... but I still feel like I'm totally alone. I tried to think about why. It's not like I don't have friends — I do, but I'm just missing having a friend I can really talk to.

Olivia has been gone for a month and a half, and I haven't had a best friend to hang with. I guess that could be it, but it feels like more than that. I'm not sure that if Olivia was in town I'd feel any different. You see, just before she left we hadn't been getting along as well.

We used to talk every day. We'd ride horses. We'd bake cookies and make caramel corn.

We'd go to the pool in the summer and to the ice-skating rink in the winter. We'd rent movies and stay up all night talking.

Then she started to get interested in clothes and boys. She just wanted to hang out at the mall all the time, looking at cute outfits to impress the boys at school. When I confronted her about what she was up to, she told me that I was Little Miss Perfect and I should get a life. Now Olivia is gone. I don't have a best friend. And hanging out at the mall won't fill the hole.

STEPPING UP:

Being strong enough to stand up to a friend is hard, especially when you have been close. But if you feel uncomfortable about something, you need to listen. That little feeling is there to help you make good choices for yourself. Letting other people's voices drown out your inner voice usually leads to you regretting your decision.

Be strong, be independent, and you will be able to look yourself in the mirror.

LET'S TALK:

God, I'm trying to listen to your warning signs. I know you come first. I also know you put me first, even before yourself. Help me to make good choices and to find like-minded friends. Amen.

DAY 62

Computer Slave

God Says: A man is a slave to whatever has mastered him.

2 Peter 2:19

My parents think I've become addicted to my computer and have been neglecting my dog, Charlie. It's my responsibility to check on him several times a day. I have to feed him, make sure he has enough to drink, take care of his bedding, and give him plenty of exercise. Sometimes I forget and don't take care of him as well as I should.

I guess I've let my computer take over my life. It just seems like there is always something I have to do. Between my house chores, babysitting, and homework it seems like I'm always running. The only time I sit down to relax is with my computer. I have to admit I spend more time than I should looking up stuff and chatting with my friends. I guess maybe I've let this computer begin to own me, instead of me owning it.

The reality is no one but Charlie dances for me when I walk in the room. When I'm bummed he cuddles up close. He's always happy just to spend time with me.

So, I'm thinking my parents are right. Maybe I do need to change some things. I'll just spend time writing my blog to you, God. Then I'll start giving myself a set time to check email and not let myself get sucked into all the other junk.

I'm off to take Charlie for a walk.

STEPPING UP:

Some things are so much fun that it becomes almost unbearable to pull yourself away. If you see yourself thinking about one thing to the exclusion of almost everything else, it's time to put on the brakes. God wants you to have a balance of many things — time spent with him, your family, friends, school, chores, pets, and fun. Pay attention to the things that consume your time, your thoughts, and your energy. You will be happier and healthier if you are balanced.

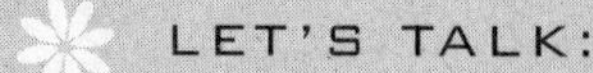

LET'S TALK:

Heavenly Father, you are Lord over all things on earth and in heaven. Forgive me when I get swept up with my computer and forget about my responsibilities. Help me to remember to always put you at the front of my thoughts and my life. Amen.

DAY 63

Bashed!

God Says: For if you forgive men when they sin against you, your heavenly Father will also forgive you.

Matthew 6:14

Last week this girl named Brittany bashed me on her blog. She said I was a stuck-up goody-goody just because I didn't go to one of the after-school parties. Then she opened up her blog to the readers asking for comments. Of course the sharks saw blood and wrote all kinds of things about me, some true and some untrue. When I read them I wanted to crawl in bed and hide. I really had a hard time making myself go to school the next day. I'm not sure when I've ever felt quite so alone and angry. I really felt hatred toward "Brittany and Friends."

Now this week, for whatever reason, Brittany is acting all nice towards me. I feel like I'm on stage, and everyone is watching to see how this is all going to play out.

I've really had to bite my tongue and not say all the mean things that have been boiling inside of me for the past week. I've had to realize that Christ would never return mean for mean.

So, I asked Brittany if we could talk, just the two of us. I told her I didn't understand why she bashed me. I said that if she was upset with me, that I wish she had spoken to me directly instead of posting mean things on her blog.

Brittany said, "It was no big deal. Get over it — it was so last week."

I asked her how she would feel if she were in my shoes, and she just rolled her eyes and told me to get a life.

I emailed Olivia and she said to let it go unless I want to get bashed by Brittany again. It's not like she said she was sorry, or she was wrong, or that she won't bash me again. I guess I need to let it go. I said what I needed to say. Now I think I'll say a prayer for Brittany.

STEPPING UP:

If you find yourself being cyber-bullied, the most important thing you can do is to talk to an adult you trust — like a parent or a teacher — right away. They can help protect you from the bullies. And don't ever go to the site where you've been bashed again — you don't need your head filled with vicious lies and rumors.

It might seem impossible at the time, but we are called to forgive the people who hurt us. That doesn't mean you have to be a bully's best friend or set yourself up for more bullying, but ask God to help you forgive just as he forgave you.

LET'S TALK:

Lord, please help me to forgive just as you forgive me. Give me wisdom and guidance in my choices of friends. Amen.

DAY 64

Admit It!

God Says: We know that the law is spiritual; but I am unspiritual, sold as a slave to sin. I do not understand what I do. For what I want to do I do not do, but what I hate I do.

Romans 7:14 – 15

Sorry. It's been a while since I last wrote. I've told myself it's because I'm so busy with school, homework, babysitting, chores, and my friends that I haven't had time. But that's not true. The truth is I've been feeling bad about myself and haven't wanted to face you, God. I miss Olivia and having a best friend here to share things with. I guess I'm lonely, and instead of reaching out to Melody and Mom, I push them away.

This morning I realized something huge. The less I talk to you, the more I do things that I know aren't making you very happy with me. It isn't like I mean to snipe at my sister, or talk back to my mother. It just happens. Afterwards I feel horrible, and wish I could take it all back. You'd think that would make me be quick to apologize, but I hate to admit I was wrong. I'm not proud of my stubbornness. It just seems to rule me sometimes, making me feel even worse.

Feeling rotten about myself and not being willing to ask for forgiveness is like an inner tug-of-war. By the time I get to blog with you I don't have much to say, you already know what's going on in my life.

I really hate it when I think that you, my true best friend, are disappointed in me. I want to be the kind of person that makes you smile.

STEPPING UP:

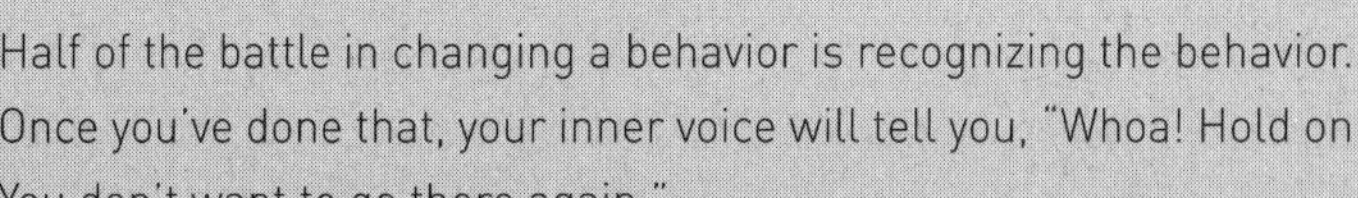

Half of the battle in changing a behavior is recognizing the behavior. Once you've done that, your inner voice will tell you, "Whoa! Hold on! You don't want to go there again."

Everyone slips sometimes, even when the inner voice is trying to be heard. That's just being human. The great thing is that God is willing to forgive and forget.

LET'S TALK:

God, I'm sorry when I go missing in action. It always amazes me that you love me in spite of myself. I really am blessed that you're always here — arms open to forgive me and welcome me back. Amen.

DAY 65

Out of Nice!

God Says: But for that very reason I was shown mercy so that in me, the worst of sinners, Christ Jesus might display his unlimited patience as an example for those who would believe on him and receive eternal life.

1 Timothy 1:16

Do you ever feel like you've just reached maximum capacity and run out of nice?

I was babysitting today. I really love the kid I babysit for, but sometimes he's a real piece of work. We always do our homework first and then we play catch. His mother is big into fresh-air activities.

Anyway, today he came in the door and immediately got on the computer to play one of his race-car games. I got him his after-school snack and told him to finish up so we could get his homework done. Well, that kid did everything under the sun to avoid doing his homework. He ate at a snail's pace. I had to drag him off the computer. He went into the bathroom and locked the door and told me to go home because he could take care of himself. It was like an alien took over his body.

By the time his mother came home I was ready to scream!

The bad thing was that Mrs. Wiard walked in looking like she could have burst into tears. She said a bunch of people were laid off at work today. So the last thing I wanted to do was to crab about her kid. I asked her if she wanted me to stay a little longer so she could unwind. She jumped at the opportunity and disappeared into her bedroom. In the meantime, the alien and I went outside to play catch.

STEPPING UP:

Everyone has limits. Even the people who push our buttons have limits to their ability to stay on an even keel. When people act out of character, it usually means something isn't right in their world. The next time you're in a situation where things aren't going well, stop, take a deep breath, and ask what's different and why. Taking the time to figure things out will help everyone get back on track.

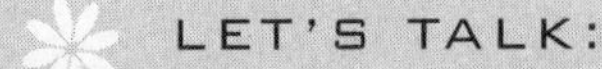

LET'S TALK:

Dear Father, I ask that you give me that patience and sensitivity to perform well in all areas of my life. Thank you for letting me see beyond my own limits to have compassion for others. Amen.

DAY 66

Make a Difference

God says: No longer will violence be heard in your land, nor ruin or destruction within your borders, but you will call your walls Salvation and your gates Praise.

Isaiah 60:18

I'm scared. Every night when I check my email, news headlines flash in bold colors announcing fighting and wars in other countries. There are news videos of people wishing Americans death and destruction. Kidnappings and murders have become everyday news. If I read or watch too much I have bad dreams of cities being blown off the face of the earth or my school being under siege by some whacked-out kid or my sister being kidnapped and my family searching for her.

So I try to click on my email before the news has a chance to jump in my face. But I still find out what's going on in the world every time I turn on the radio, or pass the living room when my parents are watching the news. All I want is for this crazy hatefulness to stop!

God, sometimes it's hard to remember that you are here walking by my side. I know you didn't say our time here was going to be an easy ride, and that's why you gave us the promise of heaven. But sometimes I just wish there was something I could do to try to make things better.

Our pastor said, "Change happens one person at a time." Maybe I need to begin by seeing what I can do to make this world a peaceful place. I'm going to talk to my parents today and ask them if we can come up with a family plan for making a difference. We could definitely start today — one neighborhood at a time!

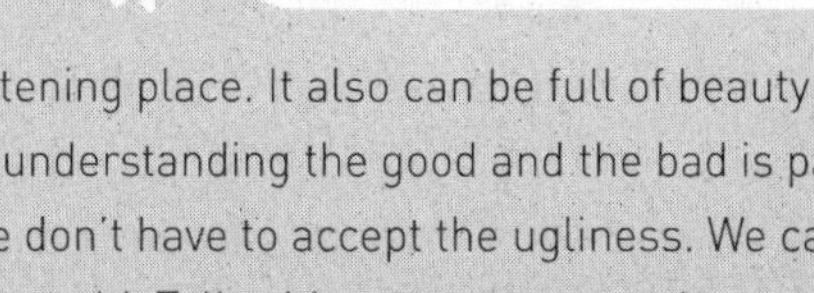

STEPPING UP:

The world can be a frightening place. It also can be full of beauty and wonder. Seeing and understanding the good and the bad is part of being an adult. But we don't have to accept the ugliness. We can do things to improve this world. Talk with your parents and come up with a plan of action. In the meantime, work on making your world a place of kindness.

And remember: if disturbing images or videos are popping up on your computer, ask your parents to adjust the privacy settings. You can be informed about the world without filling your head with garbage!

LET'S TALK:

My heavenly Father, I am so grateful that I never have to face the world alone. It's good to know you walk by my side. Sometimes I feel so insignificant. How can I do anything about this mess our world is in? Then I remember that Jesus, alone, made a difference that will be felt for eternity.

Lord, give me the wisdom and strength to do whatever I can to make this world a better place. Amen.

DAY 67

Searching for Peace

God Says: You shall not steal.

Exodus 20:15

Shopping at the mall has always been one of my favorite things to do with my mom and Melody. We spend the whole day darting in and out of dressing rooms and stopping at the food court for lunch. Sometimes we sit and people-watch. Believe me, there is never a dull moment. One of our favorite things to do is to challenge each other to score the best bargain of the day, or find the sweetest accessory.

Now I want to hurl every time I think of the mall. Yesterday while Melody and I were trying on jeans I saw a person in the next stall shove a store t-shirt in her purse that was sitting on the floor. I never should have left the store without telling. But I didn't. Even though I didn't steal the shirt myself, I know I should have talked to a manager.

Every time I think about it my heart feels like it's going to pound right out of my chest. I want to go back in time so I can make a difference. I should have gone and gotten the store manager and had them talk to the girl as she left the fitting room.

I just got so flustered. I don't even know what she looked like. All I could see was her purse, her tennis shoes, and the bottoms of her jeans. But if I had moved more quickly maybe I wouldn't feel so bad.

I'm going to talk to my mom. She'll know how to help me work through this situation.

STEPPING UP:

Stealing is a crime. If you see a theft, you're responsible to report it to an adult.

LET'S TALK:

Lord, grant me the courage to do what is right at all times, even if no one is watching. Help me to honor you by taking responsibility and standing up for the truth.

DAY 68

Prayer At The Pole

God Says: Don't let anyone look down on you because you are young, but set an example for the believers in speech, in life, in love, in faith and in purity.

1 Timothy 4:12

Our youth group decided to join the national See You at the Pole. As in, meet you at the flagpole to pray. One of the kids heard about it and showed us some clips from YouTube and Myspacetv.com. SYATP isn't something new. It was started by some kids in Texas twenty years ago, and now it's spread all over the United States. The whole deal is that SYATP is run by students, for students, to get kids praying.

We've been handing out flyers all week. That's been great and awful at the same time. A lot of kids are like, "Cool! I'm there." Others shake their heads and say things like "Get a life!" I respond by saying "I have a life with Jesus," but most of those kids roll their eyes and call me a Jesus freak.

One of the teachers told me, "Thanks for organizing this. We teachers wish we could be more verbal about things like this, but we'd lose our jobs."

"How sad is that?" I told her. "Not to worry. We've got it covered. But it would be great to see you at the pole."

Well, SYATP went on as scheduled today. It was amazing. I don't think I've ever seen the jocks, the geeks, the goths, the sk8trs, the popular, the unpopular, all standing, hand in hand, praying. The music was great, and from now on I know I have friends in Christ in every group here at school. It sure makes me look at people in a whole new way.

STEPPING UP:

Christians come in all shapes, sizes, and groups. See You at the Pole is a wonderful way to get to find each other. But even better is the fact that other people will have seen you at the pole praying, and that opens the door for them to ask you questions. What a great way to share your faith.

SYATP can be the beginning of other cool things, like a breakdown of cliques, a faith-sharing group, or a Random Acts of Kindness Team.

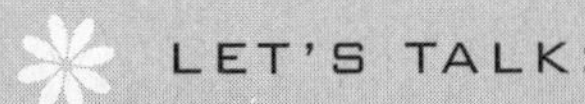

LET'S TALK:

Dear Lord, thank you for being present when I pray. Use me to break down barriers between Christians, and help all your children to be united in you. Amen.

DAY 69

Yearbook Staff

God Says: For everything in the world—the cravings of sinful man, the lust of the eyes and the boasting of what he has and does—comes not from the Father but from the world. 1 John 2:16

I joined the yearbook committee, and it's totally cool. Not only do I get a pass to walk around the school taking pictures, but I also get out of Pre-Algebra on Fridays. I just have to write captions for the pictures I've taken. How easy is that?

We're going to be posting the yearbook on the school web and print a paperback edition. We wanted to do the first hardcover yearbook ever, but the cost was more than our budget. I was disappointed, but we've been researching fundraising ideas so next year's yearbook will be even more stellar.

My cousin said they raised a ton of money for their drill team selling lollipops at lunch time. Well, I was online researching fundraising activities. Wham! Right away I started getting these gross pop-ups and nasty spams. All I did was type in one innocent word!

I am totally sicked out. I have all these ads for body-altering creams and dream dates with foreign girls. I can't believe something as innocent as a fundraiser could cause all this trouble. My computer is polluted with all this trash, and I don't have a clue how to get it clean.

STEPPING UP:

Many people find themselves in places on the Internet that they never expected. Fortunately, you can purchase filters that will keep inappropriate sites from coming up on your computer. There are also several free spam filters available online. And you can always notify your Internet provider of the unwanted emails. Talk to your parents about how to get rid of all the junk you're seeing.

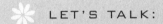

LET'S TALK:

Heavenly Father, I bet you're pretty disappointed in our world. People have taken good things like the Internet and messed it up, just like they've polluted the earth you created. I know I can't stop these people, but I'm going to be extra careful online. Amen.

DAY 70

Games

God Says: Let everyone call urgently on God. Let them give up their evil ways and their violence.

Jonah 3:8

The youth group was hanging out at Suzanne's yesterday. Everyone was there, eating pizza and messing around. Some of the kids were listening to music in the living room. We were hanging in the kitchen with Suzanne's mom. A group of boys were playing a computer game in the family room. We all were having a really good time.

Before this I never thought much about computer games and kids. I knew the games had car chases, physical fights, and sometimes gunfights, but I just never thought much about how they would affect the kids playing those games. It just never seemed like a big deal.

But today at Suzanne's I saw something that really scared me. A mellow evening turned into a kickboxing tournament. While the guys were watching the game, they got louder and rowdier. Before I knew what was happening there was a full fledged fight right in the middle of the family room! Furniture got turned over. One kid got a black eye, and Suzanne's mother called us a bunch of hoodlums and told us all to go home.

But you know what? There isn't a hoodlum in the group. Honest. We are a good group of kids. It's just some of the boys got too caught up in a game. Even while we were walking home, some of the kids kept fake-fighting. I'm thinking I don't want to be around those fighting computer games again. For now, the most competitive thing I want to do is play a game of music trivia.

STEPPING UP:

There are some wonderful things that are contagious — a smile, enthusiasm, and hope. But there are also some contagious things you want to avoid. Violence is one of them. Violent games seem innocent because they are not real. The problem is that kids imagine themselves being involved in the violence.

If you spend hours playing violent gaming, think about what is going on in your mind during all that time. Think about the things you've said during and after the game. Are these thoughts healthy and positive? Competition can be fun, but don't let it take control of you!

LET'S TALK:

Dear God, I'm not going to feed my mind and soul with anything that is ugly or harmful to your hopes and plans for me. I give you praise for all the beauty you've created in the world! Fill me with the joy of your creation. Amen.

DAY 71

Toxic Gossip

God Says: Without wood a fire goes out; without gossip a quarrel dies down.

Proverbs 26:20

I am so sick of gossip. It's everywhere! I don't know how celebrities deal. For the past year the paparazzi has hounded one of my favorite stars. She can't go anywhere without the flashing of photographers' cameras. Their whole goal is to show her every blemish, fault, and weakness. What I was afraid of happening to her has now become reality — she's having a meltdown, and who wouldn't? Seriously! Every mistake she makes is broadcast to the whole world online, on T.V., and in magazines and newspapers.

Today's first news flash was a picture of her sobbing. Man, could I relate. I've been raked over the coals a few times both online and at school. I don't get why people are so cruel. Can't they remember what it felt like to be the person people are talking about?

I read this great Bible verse today in Proverbs. It says that if you don't fuel the fire, the fire will go out. Like if you immerse yourself in gossip, that will feed the fire and keep the gossip going.

As of today, I'm not going to spend my time or money reading gossip magazines, watching gossip T.V., or searching for and reading internet gossip. I've already stopped wasting my time in computer chat rooms where the gossip flies. Maybe I can challenge my friends to a gossip-free zone?

STEPPING UP:

Gossip is an age-old problem, but it doesn't mean you have to take part. The best way to handle gossip is not to participate. Don't listen to gossip, and don't pass along the information. Tell the school gossip she should think about how she would feel if people were talking trash about her. Then walk away.

LET'S TALK:

Dear Father, I know you hate gossip. Help me to treat everyone with the same sensitivity and respect I want from them, and help me to glorify you through every word I speak. Amen.

DAY 72

Power Down

God Says: Be still, and know that I am God.

Psalm 46:10

We had our first major winter storm last night. It began with ice coating all the branches and progressed to whopper snowflakes like paper doilies. In the morning everything was coated with over a foot of snow and we found ourselves without power. School was closed, and the radio said not to go out unless it was an emergency.

It was so weird. No television, no computer, no heat, none of the modern conveniences. Our oven and stove top wouldn't work. We had to keep the fridge closed because Mom was worried about the food spoiling. Dad laughed and said we could always put the stuff outside.

Our house was getting cold so Dad built a fire. We all dressed in layers and cuddled up by the fireplace. The only sounds were coming from the crackling of burning logs. All of the usual noise had been silenced by the storm.

I don't remember us ever sitting like that. No one spoke. We all just enjoyed the quiet and being together. Later when we were hungry we cooked over the open fire. We played board games and then read our favorite verses from the Bible. The power came back on around 7:15 tonight, and I have to say I was almost sorry to go back to our noisy lives. I'll never forget this day.

STEPPING UP: 

Our lives are noisy, overscheduled, and taxing. We as a society have forgotten how to take a day of rest. Sometimes it is good to just shut everything off and be still.

Spend some time today reflecting on life, talking to God, and enjoying his world.

 LET'S TALK:

Thank you, God, for the gift of rest. Help me to find times of quiet and stillness when I can listen for your voice. Amen.

DAY 73

Same Difference

God Says: Then make my joy complete by being like-minded, having the same love, being one in spirit and purpose. Philippians 2:2

Our youth group has connected with youth groups from all over the Unites States. We have five sister churches that we stay in contact with. We've challenged their youth groups to some pretty great ministry stuff, like who can clock the most hours at the soup kitchens or collect the most books for kids who have never owned a book. We also put together shoeboxes full of stuff for kids in South America and Africa.

What is totally cool is chatting online with youth groups from all over the USA on a private forum. I love hearing about other people in other states and how they live their lives. What they do when they hang out, what they eat when they're together, and what kinds of things they can do because of where they live, like snowmobile or surf.

What I'm realizing from different youth group chat rooms is that people are the same all over this world. Sure, peoples' traditions and favorite foods may differ depending on if they live in Chicago and love pizza or the Southwest and eat TexMex. But in the end, the stuff we talk about is pretty much the same. We all want to have friends. We love doing service projects and challenging the other youth groups. The great thing is that while we have fun meeting each other's challenges, the ministries benefit so many people.

STEPPING UP:

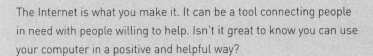

The Internet is what you make it. It can be a tool connecting people in need with people willing to help. Isn't it great to know you can use your computer in a positive and helpful way?

LET'S TALK:

Thank you, God, for the tools you give us to communicate and learn more about each other. Help me to take advantage of these opportunities and to use them to bring you glory. Amen.

DAY 74

Tricked? or Talented?

God Says: Keep me from the snares they have laid for me, from the traps set by evildoers.

Psalm 141:9

When I was online last week I saw a contest looking for talented writers. They had a story starter and then allowed you 1,000 words to finish the story. Writing has always been such a breeze for me. I realized I was good at writing when my teachers began reading my writing in class. I used to pretend I was a famous journalist reporting all the neighborhood news for publication in DAILY DIARY. Then, when I started taking pictures, I knew I was destined for being a photojournalist, like for *National Geographic*.

Anyway, I submitted an entry for the contest and heard back a day later. I was so pumped! They told me that I totally rocked! They also said that for a small fee I could have an agent review my entry. Mom said OK. I waited, and then in a few days I got another letter from an editor. He said that the story was good, and that for another small fee he would line edit and make suggestions for a rewrite. I agreed, and two days later my story came back with a whole list of suggestions and another request for money to review the revision.

This whole thing started out without any mention of money. Now every time I turn around they want more and more. I am beginning to wonder if they really think I'm a good writer, or if this is a scam.

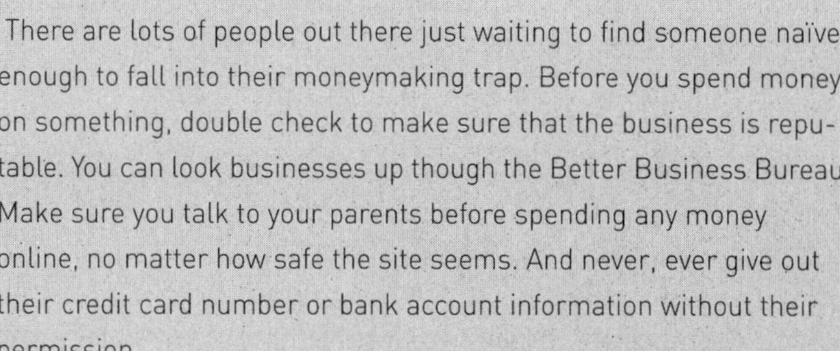

STEPPING UP:

There are lots of people out there just waiting to find someone naïve enough to fall into their moneymaking trap. Before you spend money on something, double check to make sure that the business is reputable. You can look businesses up though the Better Business Bureau. Make sure you talk to your parents before spending any money online, no matter how safe the site seems. And never, ever give out their credit card number or bank account information without their permission.

LET'S TALK:

Dear God, it's so frustrating when good tools are used for evil purposes. Help me remember that you are in control, and keep me safe from situations in which someone tries to take advantage of me. Give me a clear mind to spot disasters before they appear. Amen.

DAY 75

Secret Screen Names

God Says: The Lord is faithful, and he will strengthen and protect you from the evil one.

2 Thessalonians 3:3

Oof! It's been a pretty busy week, and today was no exception. I had a yearbook meeting for an hour after school and then had to run to get to my babysitting job on time. Mrs. Wiard was late getting home, so I had to run all the way home to be back in time for dinner. And then I had a mountain of homework to get through. Once I finished, I decided to get on the computer and see who else was online. I logged into instant messenger while I was checking my email, and after a few minutes I was chatting with a few different people from school.

All of a sudden a screen name came up that I didn't think I recognized. It was really similar to Chloe's, so I clicked "accept" to see what was going on. It was this girl from school — at least she talked like someone from my school. She asked me how classes were going and everything, but the weird thing is that she wouldn't tell me her name. She would just go "LOL" whenever I asked. And then she asked for my phone number and address because she wanted to study together sometime. I got really creeped out and signed off without saying anything else.

I talked to Dad about it, and he said that it almost certainly wasn't someone from school who wanted to hang out. He told me that there are really dangerous people who might pretend to be someone I know in order to get information about me — like my phone number and where I live. I'm going to be more careful with who I give my screen name to from now on — I don't want anyone I don't trust to be able to find me!

STEPPING UP:

It's a sad fact that not everyone online is a safe person to be around. There are lots of criminals, called "online predators," who scour the internet trying to find information that they could use to hurt you. This is why it's super important to protect your identity. Never give out any personal information to someone on the computer that you can't see face-to-face. You never know how that information might be used.

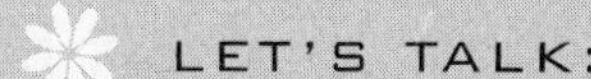

LET'S TALK:

Dear Lord, it's scary to think of someone I don't even know trying to hurt me. Please keep me safe and protect me from all evil. Amen.

DAY 76

Please Don't Fight

God Says: Let us therefore make every effort to do what leads to peace and to mutual edification.

Romans 14:19

My parents had a huge fight tonight. I've never heard them fight like that. Sure, they disagree about things, but they've never had a screaming match like this before. In the past when they disagreed, they told us to go outside and shoot some hoops or go to our room. But tonight they just let it all loose. That's why I'm feeling scared.

The fight started when Mom asked Dad about something on their online bank statement. I know money has been tight. Dad's company is downsizing and everyone who was kept on had to take a pay cut. Dad sat us down and told us we were all going to have to be careful about how we spent money. He talked to us about budgeting for things like groceries and turning off lights and not taking half-hour showers.

I know Mom has been watching every penny. She's been adding hours to her part-time job. We've been packing lunches and haven't been making after-school stops for ice cream. We've cut back on buying magazines, and Mom's been talking about changing our Internet server to a cheaper one.

I really hate that money has gotten so tight that we have to worry about bills. I don't want my parents to fight. I want things back to normal.

STEPPING UP:

No one likes to deal with money problems, but they are a reality of the world we live in. God calls us to be good stewards of the resources he's given us, which means not spending frivolously or begging parents to buy you something they can't afford.

LET'S TALK:

Dear Father, money can be such a headache. I hate it when it causes problems that I don't know how to solve. Help me to always lean on you when I'm scared and don't know where to turn. Amen.

DAY 77

Making the Grade

God Says: Whatever you do, work at it with all your heart.

Colossians 3:23

I totally feel like I'm under a magnifying glass! And it's all because we've joined the 21st century with our school technology! Our school has a website where our teachers can post our grades and leave comments on a daily basis. Each family is given their own space with a private entry code so the parents can't ever say they weren't given the information before a child fails a class. Teachers are still supposed to contact the parents in case of an academic emergency, and parents can email the teacher with any concerns they might have.

I forgot my homework the other day, and I was caught text messaging one of my friends during math yesterday. My teacher emailed my parents, and today after school we all had to meet. They were talking like I wasn't even in the room! My teacher even said this was an academic emergency!

At first I didn't think it was that big of a deal. But when I saw the disappointment on my parents' face and the concern on my teacher's face I realized maybe I needed to step up to my slacking.

So I said, "Ok. I messed up. I promise I won't carry my phone during school. And I will not miss any more homework. I realize I was getting sloppy about my school responsibilities and it won't happen again."

Both my teacher and my parents were just sitting there. Finally Dad said, "All right then. We all understand what needs to happen. Thanks for calling us all together," and we drove home. On the way, Dad said that he was going to be taking away my phone for two weeks.

I really don't like the feeling of disappointing my parents or you, God. So I'm going to use the brain I've been given and behave in a manor that is honorable to you, my parents, and myself.

STEPPING UP: 

Parents know that little things have a way of becoming habits and bad habits can keep you from reaching your goals. Think about a snowball. It starts out the size of a baseball, but keep it rolling and you've got yourself the start of an avalanche!
Remember that the little things do count, because they're what form your habits, and your habits are what form your character.

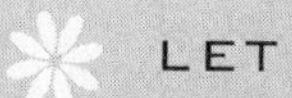 LET'S TALK:

Dear God, help me to always work with integrity, never slacking off or taking shortcuts. Keep me active and productive in the pursuit of your plan for me! Amen.

DAY 78

Thanksgiving Parade

God Says: Be joyful always; pray continually; give thanks in all circumstances, for this is God's will for you in Christ Jesus.

1 Thessalonians 5:16 – 18

We just had Thanksgiving, and besides being stuffed, I'm thinking that the whole day had more to do with the parade and food than taking time to give you thanks, God.

The morning started with my whole family parading downstairs to watch the parade on TV. Then there was the relative parade, which started about an hour before the actual dinner. All the aunts and uncles and cousins started parading in with their arms full of pies, salads, veggies, and sweet potatoes. They placed everything on the table in preparation for the food parade, then paraded though the kitchen to smell what was cooking. When the turkey was done, everyone lined up to parade though the food line.

Finally when the whole gang sat down, Dad said grace, and a nanosecond after that we all jumped into eating and talking. Then the parading began again with a line snaking by the dessert table. The grand finale was the big parade to the TV for football!

So I've been thinking that I didn't really take time out to think about all I've got to be thankful for. I really am grateful for my family, for all those parading relatives, for food, and the memories we shared today. I'm sorry I didn't show you that today, God. But I guess it's never too late, huh? So thanks, God, for a fun day and a good life. I'm full of THANKSgiving to you!

STEPPING UP:

Holidays are chaotic — no questions about it. We worry so much about how many different pies we should have and whether our team will win the big game that we forget the real meaning of Thanksgiving. Thanksgiving is supposed to be just that — a time of THANKSGIVING. There are many great ideas you can find on the Internet by typing in Thanksgiving traditions. A great one is passing around a plate with five kernels of corn on it. As the plate is passed, each person shares five things for which he or she is grateful. Start searching now so you'll be ready for next year.

LET'S TALK:

Dear Heavenly Father, you've done some pretty cool things for me and my family, and I just want to say thanks. I know I'm blessed, and I am very grateful. Help me to keep your love and grace in the front of my thoughts, even when things go crazy. Amen.

DAY 79

Back It Up!

God Says: His work will be shown for what it is, because the Day will bring it to light. It will be revealed with fire, and the fire will test the quality of each man's work.

1 Corinthians 3:13

I've been crazy busy researching volcanoes in the world, especially Vesuvius, for a school report. I'm really interested in that volcano because I have relatives who live in a little town across the gulf of Naples, in Italy.

I've taken all my research and family information and have been entering it all day on my computer. Everything was going smoothly. Then the power went out while I was working, and I'd forgotten to save, save, save as I was writing. I lost half of my report. I could just scream. My report is due in the morning, and I'm going to be up half the night rewriting what I lost of my paper.

I'm feeling pretty cranky — mostly at myself. I got wrapped up in writing and forgot to take the time to back up my work. Now because I was rushing through, I have to put in even more time. Lord, I know this is one of those lessons that I needed to learn. I need to slow down and take time to do the best I can the first time. You certainly didn't rush when you were creating the world. You took a day, did some creating, then looked to see that it was good before you went on to the next creation. Man, do I need to take a lesson from you!

STEPPING UP:

It is so easy to get into "the zone" when you're writing. Remembering to stop and save your work is simple to do and well worth the seconds it takes to do it. It's also important to keep another copy of your work, either on a flash drive or an external hard drive.

But sometimes despite our best intentions, we still make mistakes. How you handle those glitches and frustrations is just as important. Take a deep breath. Learn from the mistake. And get back to work.

LET'S TALK:

Dear God, it is an awesome thing to create something. I thank you that you are a creator and that you made us in your image to be creative. Lord, help me to take the time necessary to create and see that it is good. Also, God, help me to have a good attitude when things go wrong. Amen.

DAY 80

Believing Is the Key

God Says: Always be prepared to give an answer to everyone who asks you to give the reason for the hope that you have.

1 Peter 3:15

Last week on the bus the girl next to me said she knew she was getting into heaven because she was a good person. I knew she needed Jesus, but I didn't know how to say it or what verses I could show her. So I didn't say anything.

Then, that night our youth group leader started a debate club. Our youth leaders act like unbelievers in the debate, and then we have to counter their misinformation with what we've memorized. So the first thing we had to do was research about what we believe as Christians and why. There are, like, a million websites where you can look up Bible verses, Bible topics, and Bible study. Who knew? I found all kinds of verses, like 1 John 5:10–12, Acts 4:12, John 14:6, John 1:12–13, and John 3:16, plus so much more.

But this whole defending Jesus thing isn't the same as

Jesus. I'm not sure I want to try and make her know

maybe the best way is to let her see Jesus

actions. So I'm thinking of ways to do

her to our Youth Group Christmas

Box party. We have a night where we pack shoe boxes for the homeless. We put in gloves, hats, socks, long underwear, granola bars, a water bottle, a toothbrush, toothpaste, a bar of soap, and a note to tell them they are loved by Jesus. We eat pizza and listen to Christmas carols. It's totally cool and a great way to share Christ.

STEPPING UP:

Taking time to know the Word will serve you well, not only in being able to defend your faith, but also as a daily guide on how to make wise choices. When searching online, be sure to stay with search engines that are reputable. Check the verses against what you have in your own Bible at home. Once you've found a few good sources, bookmark those sites for future reference. But always remember the best way to let someone know Christ is to be his reflection in who you are and what you do.

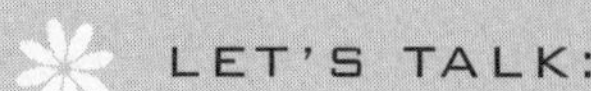

LET'S TALK:

Dear God, thank you for putting people in my life who challenge me and help me learn about you. Thank you for your Word and all it teaches me about living in faith. Make me a living example of how you work in the lives of your children. Amen.

DAY 81

She Likes Me ... She Likes Me Not

God Says: A friend loves at all times.

Proverbs 17:17

I am so upset. Rachel and I got into a humungous fight, and it totally wasn't my fault! She kept calling me, like, every hour on the hour, wanting me to come over. My parents wouldn't let me leave the house because my cousins were in town from Pennsylvania. Then Rachel kept calling me wanting to know everything I was doing. Mom had a fit because I was on my cell so much. I tried to explain to Rachel that if she called me one more time my mother was going to take my phone away, but she still called a half hour later and I answered even though Mom had told me not to. My mother totally freaked and took my phone, and now I'm grounded for a week.

The next day at school, Rachel was really nasty to me. She called me a major loser and told me that I wasn't her friend anymore. She said that friends don't ignore each other.

I wasn't ignoring her. My parents said it was rude to be on the phone while I had company. So now Rachel won't talk to me. She's even blocked me from her blog. I can't believe this is happening. What happened to friends forever?

My mom heard me crying and asked me what was wrong. I told her what had happened with Rachel. She told me friends sometimes aren't really friends. She asked me what I thought was more important, listening to your parents or the demands of a friend? Was it more important to talk on the phone with a friend I see every day at school or spend time with a cousin I hardly ever see and really enjoy? We talked for a long time. I felt better by the time she left.

STEPPING UP:

There is a time and a place for cell phone use. A good rule to remember is to be considerate to the people you are with by not talking on the phone. That way you let the people you are with know they are important to you. Put your phone on silent and take care of calls when your time is free.

LET'S TALK:

Lord, please guide me. Help me to be the kind of daughter you would have me be and a friend someone like me would like to have. I know you have a plan for me. Amen.

DAY 82

Grounded

God Says: No discipline seems pleasant at the time, but painful. Later on, however, it produces a harvest of righteousness and peace for those who have been trained by it.
Hebrews 12:11

I guess I shouldn't be complaining. I totally deserve to be punished. My mom told me not to talk on the phone and I did anyway. I disobeyed her even after being warned, and I was rude to my cousin. I am so upset with myself.

The worst part is that I got myself grounded during the Ice Festival. For three days everyone in town hangs out at the square. There are ice carving expositions, log cutting contests, and homemade ice cream. They build a temporary ice rink under the stars and decorate its rim with twinkling Christmas lights. The stores on the square have open house parties with delicious treats, and there are bands playing in the gazebo. And I have to miss it all!

My parents have always been very clear about what they expect me to do — to always follow the Ten Commandments. I know it's their job to discipline me. I'm really, really disappointed in myself that I let them and you down. And I realize I let myself down too. I made a choice — a bad choice — not to follow my mother's instructions, and now I have to give up doing something I really enjoy.

I'm going to have to miss the Ice Festival this year. But I promise you this — I'll be there next year for sure.

STEPPING UP:

Missing out on something you look forward to gives you a chance not only to think about your past choices, but also your future choices. Time being disciplined gives God a chance to work in your heart.

LET'S TALK:

Dear Father, thank you for being a forgiving God who loves me even when I mess up. I also want to thank you for giving me my parents. They love me like you love me — unconditionally. Amen.

DAY 83

Unlock the Chains!

God Says: Do not share in the sins of others. Keep yourself pure.

1 Timothy 5:22

I received one of those chain letters today. It had a prayer in it, and the prayer was absolutely beautiful. It asked the reader to say this prayer for our troops. There were some awesome photographs of men and women in the service helping people and pictures of a circle of servicemen praying together, followed by photos of the wounded. The American flag waved in the background as music played.

The forwarded email really pulled at my heart. I have a cousin fighting in Iraq, so this email made me want to send it on to everyone I have on my list. But then I read on to the bottom. The note at the end made me crazy mad. They took a good thing, saying a prayer for our troops, and trashed it by adding something like: If you send this on to 5 people, you are patriotic. If you pass it on to 100 people, you could be president, and if you don't pass this on you are a major loser and something bad will happen!

It was beyond stupid. I think chain letters ought to be outlawed. All they ever do is try to manipulate a person to do what the sender wants. I'll pray for the troops just like I always do, but I won't be sending on any chain letter garbage.

STEPPING UP:

Chain letters are a drain on everyone they come in contact with. They clog up the Internet. They fill up your email, and they can carry viruses to your computer. You're wise not to open a forward, or a chain letter. If you recognize the sender, email them asking if the information forwarded is life or death information. If the forward isn't important, ask them not to send forwards to you in the future.

LET'S TALK:

Dear God, give me wisdom and discernment as I read emails and communicate with my friends. Help me not to get bogged down in untruths, but to always seek out what is genuine. Amen.

DAY 84

Picture This

God Says: Humble yourselves, therefore, under God's mighty hand, that he may lift you up in due time.

1 Peter 5:6

I've just seen some of the finished pages for the yearbook, and I am speechless. Seriously, I took all these amazing pictures, then spent hours working in a photo-editing program to create some unforgettable montages, some sweet single shots, and some picture-perfect team shots. I'm telling you, I ought to get some kind of photo award. I worked double hard making sure every group in school was represented. And believe me, that wasn't easy. Then, on top of that, I had to come up with catchy captions to go along with each picture. The captions needed to be funny but not mean.

Anyway, so I see the credits page, and it starts with the editor, then the editorial assistants, the teacher advisors, the subscriptions editor, the marketing head, the creative director, and even the cafeteria cook. My name isn't mentioned anywhere. What is that about?

I realize I'm new this year, but I've added a lot to this yearbook. Think about it. What's a yearbook without awesome pictures? "So," I ask the editor, "what's with no mention of me, your main photographer?" She tells me to get over it. She says, "The photographer is always mentioned in the back before the advertisers."

I'm thinking I must need a lesson in pride. Seems like pride is one of those things that you, Lord, talk a lot about in Proverbs. Like Proverbs 29:23, "A man's pride brings him low, but a man of lowly spirit gains honor." So maybe my photographs are meant to speak for themselves without a big recognition in the yearbook.

STEPPING UP:

It's a harsh reality that you won't always get credit for something you've worked on. Sometimes, that's just part of being a team, when everyone works together to make a product or win a game. Take pride in being part of the team and having made good contributions, and be confident that your work will get noticed!

LET'S TALK:

Dear Father, I know your desire for us is that we should be humble. I really don't want it to be all about me. Forgive me when I desire all the credit, and help me to take joy in the talents you've given me. Always let me honor you with my work, because it's not about me—it's about you. Amen.

DAY 85

Accessory Regret

God Says: Why spend money on what is not bread, and your labor on what does not satisfy? Listen, listen to me, and eat what is good, and your soul will delight in the richest of fare.
Isaiah 55:2

My closet was beginning to look like a fashion disaster, so I started doing some research online for helpful suggestions and found a list of great ideas for salvaging my clothes. The main suggestion was adding accessories to your regulars. They had some awesome style suggestions on how to use a belt on an old shirt to give it a funky fresh look, adding jeweled pins to shirts, purses, and belts for a little glitz, and how ribbons, bows, or scarves give a feminine touch. They said shoes make an outfit, and a couple articles gave great suggestions for finding buys online.

I didn't have to pay for a whole new closet of clothes — which is great, since I don't have that much from my babysitting and I can't ask my parents for money right now! I got online and started putting all these really inexpensive fashion accessories in my online cart. I ordered a scarf for $6.00 and bangle bracelets for $7.50. I found three great belt, purse, and shoe sets. The prices were phenomenal. And last but not least, I scored some dazzling pins.

Everything was so cheap. Except when I totaled the bill, I totally freaked. It was just a few dollars here and a few dollars there. How did it add up to so much?

I showed my mom and she gasped. She emptied the cart and told me to grab my purse — we were going thrift store shopping. She was going to show me how to find beautiful things while staying within my budget, and still have some money left to put in the mission box.

STEPPING UP:

Self-control when it comes to buying great fashion is hard enough, let alone when you find a great deal. Always start with a budget, which is your available cash. Subtract the amount of each purchase from your available cash. Every time you subtract the cost of a purchased item, you have a new and lesser amount of available cash. When your cash runs low, it's time to stop buying. That way there won't be any surprises when the bills come in.

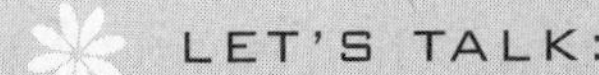

LET'S TALK:

Dear Lord, give me the self-control and wisdom to spend wisely. Teach me to be a good steward of the blessings you have given me. Amen.

DAY 86

Stop Hating!

God Says: Do not hate your brother in your heart.

Leviticus 19:17

Hate. People use the word everyday. I hate math. I hate brussels sprouts. I hate...

I was totally shocked when the school chat room started talking HATE. Not hate of things. Hate of people. Just because of their differences.

It all began because of the news about a gang of kids beating up an innocent bystander because of his color. The headlines were everywhere — online, on the news, and in the paper.

Our principal decided to have an assembly on tolerance. She said we needed to take an active role in preventing hate crimes. She felt an education in tolerance was what would change the world, one person at a time. The assembly really got me thinking.

How can good people — even people who say they're Christians — hold such hatred in their hearts?

I can't believe that the people I attend school with could ever be so cruel, but hate crimes can happen anywhere. What an eye-opener. Well, this is one girl who's going to do what she can to help our principal. I'm going to do whatever it takes to make our school an educated, tolerant environment.

STEPPING UP: 

Learning tolerance begins when people see others as individuals. That means people need to move outside their own groups and take the time to get to know individuals in other groups. The better we get to know people, the easier it gets to see the similarities instead of the differences.

 LET'S TALK:

Father, I pray for unity among all your children. I pray that we would learn to be one in you and to celebrate our differences instead of using them to hurt each other. Amen.

DAY 87

Tolerance Plan

God Says: Now that you have purified yourselves by obeying the truth so that you have sincere love for your brothers, love one another deeply, from the heart.

1 Peter 1:22

Who knew that people could still be so bigoted in this day and age? I guess I never even thought about it. But all of a sudden with the principal having the tolerance talk at school, the lack of tolerance of different nationalities has become a huge issue.

I went straight to the principal this morning and told her I wanted to do whatever I could to help. I told her how disgusted I was with what's been going on in the world with all the hate crimes. She told me I wasn't the only one that came to her this morning. She said she was going to have a meeting with all the students that had approached her to see how we could improve the school environment.

During 6th period we met and brainstormed some ideas. First we decided to have an assembly where everyone could participate in coming up with a tolerance plan. In the meantime we came up with a few ideas to begin with.

Biased speech and actions are unacceptable.

We are going to put together a conflict resolution team.

We made a box where students could confidentially report harassment or bullying.

We also set a date to have a school-wide open house called Celebrating Differences. Students of different nationalities will be able to get together to make food and provide information about their cultural background. I am hoping that these steps we're taking will open the hearts of the students who have been raised to hate and fear differences.

STEPPING UP:

We are a diverse nation that needs to grow in tolerance. Each and every one of us needs to work together to build an atmosphere of acceptance and love.

LET'S TALK:

Lord, I am grateful to be living in a country where the laws say we are all created equally and should be treated that way. Help me to be one person making a change in how people relate to one another. Thank you, God, for creating and loving us all equally. Amen.

DAY 88

Hello Jesus!

God Says: "Let the little children come to me, and do not hinder them, for the kingdom of heaven belongs to such as these.

Matthew 19:14

I saw an invitation in the newspaper for kids to send letters to Santa. Kids could write a letter to Santa and get a response. The paper said they would print some of the children's letters. Seeing this gave me an idea. I went to my youth group and asked if they would like to help.

I thought—why not let kids send a birthday card or letter to Baby Jesus? We would then send a card back that would include a Scripture-based story of Jesus' birth and a page to color of Jesus with the children.

The kids in my youth group liked the idea. We put a post in our church bulletin, and that very day we started getting emails and letters. I was thinking we would get a couple of letters, but it's been more like an avalanche. We're scrambling to keep up. We've also gotten letters from the parents saying thank you for offering this opportunity to remind the children of Jesus' birth being the most important gift.

Now we're even getting letters from people outside of our church, which is a good thing. I'm so excited to be able to share Christ in a different way this year!

STEPPING UP: 

Every community has different needs, but all of them share in the need to know Christ. When you come up on a major holiday, spend some time brainstorming about different ways you can share Christ's love with others.

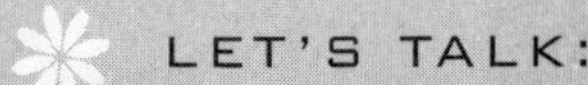

LET'S TALK:

Dear Father, thank you for the opportunity to make your love known to people in my neighborhood and all over the world. I ask for your blessing as I seek to bring your Word to people who have never known you. Amen.

DAY 89

North Pole News

God Says: Whatever you do, whether in word or deed, do it all in the name of the Lord Jesus, giving thanks to God the Father through him.

Colossians 3:17

It's almost Christmas, and my family's been going all out with the decorations. I love all our family traditions — tromping outside in the snow to cut down the tree, listening to Christmas carols and drinking hot chocolate (with extra marshmallows!) while we decorate, and putting the angel on the very tip-top of the tree. It's been so much fun to take out all the ornaments we remember from when we were younger, like the stars made of popsicle sticks and tiny mangers constructed from macaroni. My favorite part was just after Thanksgiving. Instead of going shopping like the rest of America, we made a sign with twinkle lights saying, "Jesus is the reason for the season!" I wrote a North Pole Newsletter to family and friends challenging everyone to get down to basics. I've asked everyone to be Jesus' hands.

We've decided this year we don't need piles of gifts. No shopping sprees for sweaters no one wears. This year we are going to make something — a song, a picture, a letter, coupons, cookies — the possibilities are endless. This year we're going to send letters to soldiers, and we're going to continue writing after Christmas. This year we're going to make cookies for our elderly neighbor, and take the time to visit. This year we're going to volunteer at the soup kitchen as a family on Christmas Day. This year we're going to remember Jesus is the reason for the season.

STEPPING UP:

People tend to forget what Christmas is all about. The month of December is filled with Christmas trees, ornaments, parties, cookies, gifts, wrapping paper, and financial worries. This year, use your talents to be Jesus' hands, his eyes, his ears. Show people the love of Christ through your actions.

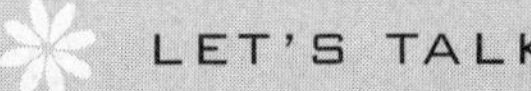

LET'S TALK:

Dear Father, thank you for special times with my family spent talking about you and all the ways you work in our lives. Help me to be your hands and feet as I seek to share you with the world. Amen.

Supper with Jesus

God Says: Thanks be to God for his indescribable gift!

2 Corinthians 9:15

This was the best Christmas Day ever. First thing this morning we added the baby Jesus to our nativity scene. We went to church, and then we came home to open presents. We made all of our gifts this year. I gave everyone one of my photographs I'd taken during the year. I used a photo-editing program and polished some great shots. I finished a photograph essay of Dad playing golf. For my mom, I took a sepia picture of her mother's hands making bread and framed it with Grandma's recipe. I gave my sister a picture I took of her making the winning basket at one of her basketball games and framed it with her jersey.

I got really great gifts too. My sister knit us all these totally sweet scarves. Dad made us these cool bulletin boards using antique frames from Grandma's house, and Mom made us cozy quilts out of our favorite old t-shirts. I loved these presents more than any other gifts I've ever received.

The afternoon was spent with people from our church providing Christmas dinner for the poor in our community. We gave everyone a Bible and sang Christmas carols.

Tonight as I sit here blogging you, God, I can't help but thank you for this time we've spent together. I know you aren't just here while I'm writing to you. I know you walk with me daily. I thank you, Lord, for sending us Jesus. Because of him I know I am forgiven for my sins, and until I can meet you in paradise, I look forward to all the times we have right here.

STEPPING UP:

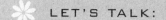

It's good for a person to have someone to talk to; someone you know loves you unconditionally any time day or night. God is that someone. You never have to worry about fitting in or being good enough. God chose you. He loves you, and he is always ready to listen.

LET'S TALK:

Father, thank you for loving me enough to send your son to die for me. Thank you for loving me even when I am unlovable. Thank you for calling me to be part of your loving family. Thank you for always being here for me. Amen.

Sophie Series

Written by Nancy Rue

Meet Sophie LaCroix, a creative soul who's destined to become a great film director someday. But many times, her overactive imagination gets her in trouble!

Book 1: Sophie's World
IBSN: 978-0-310-70756-1

Book 2: Sophie's Secret
ISBN: 978-0-310-70757-8

Book 3: Sophie Under Pressure
ISBN: 978-0-310-71840-6

Book 4: Sophie Steps Up
ISBN: 978-0-310-71841-3

Book 5: Sophie's First Dance
ISBN: 978-0-310-70760-8

Book 6: Sophie's Stormy Summer
ISBN: 978-0-310-70761-5

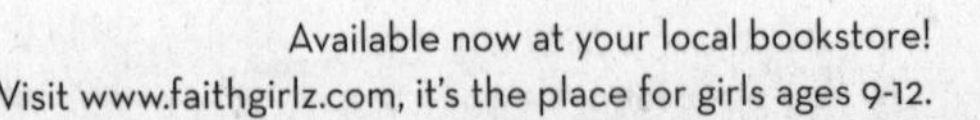
Available now at your local bookstore!
Visit www.faithgirlz.com, it's the place for girls ages 9-12.

Sophie Series

Written by Nancy Rue

Book 7: Sophie's Friendship Fiasco
ISBN: 978-0-310-71842-0

Book 8: Sophie and the New Girl
ISBN: 978-0-310-71843-7

Book 9: Sophie Flakes Out
ISBN: 978-0-310-71024-0

Book 10: Sophie Loves Jimmy
ISBN: 978-0-310-71025-7

Book 11: Sophie's Drama
ISBN: 978-0-310-71844-4

Book 12: Sophie Gets Real
ISBN: 978-0-310-71845-1

Nonfiction

Everybody Tells Me to Be Myself but I Don't Know Who I Am

ISBN 978-0-310-71295-4

This addition to the Faithgirlz! line helps girls face the challenges of being their true selves with fun activities, interactive text, and insightful tips.

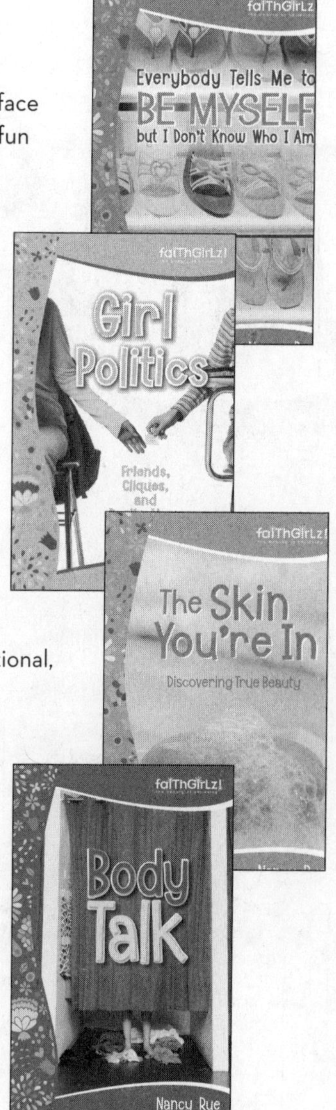

Girl Politics

ISBN 978-0-310-71296-1

Parents and kids alike may think that getting teased or arguing with friends is just part of growing up, but where is the line between normal kid stuff and harmful behavior? This book is a guide for girls on how to deal with girl politics, God-style.

The Skin You're In: Discovering True Beauty

ISBN 978-0-310-71999-1

Beauty tips and the secret of true inner beauty are revealed in this interactive, inspirational, fun addition to the Faithgirlz! line.

Body Talk

ISBN 978-0-310-71275-6

In a world where bodies are commodities, girls are under more pressure at younger ages. This book is a fun and God-centered way to give girls the facts and self-confidence they need as they mature into young women.

Available now at your local bookstore!
Visit www.faithgirlz.com, it's the place for girls ages 9-12.